The Nigerian Nightmare

MY JOURNEY OUT OF AFRICA TO THE KANSAS CITY CHIEFS AND BEYOND

The Nigerian Nightmare

MY JOURNEY OUT OF AFRICA TO THE KANSAS CITY CHIEFS AND BEYOND

Christian Okoye with Greg Hanlon

TRIUMPH
BOOKS

Library of Congress Cataloging-in-Publication Data

Names: Okoye, Christian, author. | Hanlon, Greg, author.
Title: The Nigerian nightmare: my journey out of Africa to the Kansas City
  Chiefs and beyond / Christian Okoye with Greg Hanlon.
Description: Chicago, Illinois: Triumph Books, 2023.
Identifiers: LCCN 2023016966 | ISBN 9781637272619 (cloth)
Subjects: LCSH: Okoye, Christian| Running backs (Football)—United
  States—Biography. | Nigerian Americans—Biography. | Immigrants—United
  States—Biography. | Kansas City Chiefs (Football team) |
  Football—Missouri—Kansas City—History—20th century. |
  Nigeria—History—Civil War—Personal narratives. | BISAC:
  SPORTS & RECREATION / Football | SPORTS & RECREATION /
  Track & Field
Classification: LCC GV939.O49 A3 2023 | DDC 796.332092
  [B]—dc23/eng/20230608
LC record available at https://lccn.loc.gov/2023016966

This book is available in quantity at special discounts for your group or organization. For further information, contact:
  Triumph Books LLC
  814 North Franklin Street
  Chicago, Illinois 60610
  (312) 337-0747
  www.triumphbooks.com

Printed in U.S.A.
ISBN: 978-1-63727-261-9
Design by Nord Compo
Photos courtesy of Azusa Pacific Athletics unless otherwise indicated

To Tiana, Kosi, and Laylah, you are my whole world.
I love you more than anything.

Contents

FOREWORD

It was training camp in 1989. I had just become the running backs coach for the Kansas City Chiefs under new head coach Marty Schottenheimer, and I was having one of my first meetings with my positional group. The topic was blitz pickup and the different rules for running backs depending on whether the defense was in a 4-3 front or a 3-4. Basic stuff. It's the type of stuff you establish in the first few days of camp before moving on to more complex things. But Christian Okoye had a question: "Coach, what's a 4-3 and what's a 3-4?"

We had our work cut out for us.

Fortunately, Christian was a guy with an incredible capacity for work. I coached with the Chiefs for four years from 1989 through 1992, and Christian would ask every question that he had and then listen intently. In that patient way of his, he dotted every i and crossed every t. He came a long way—fast. In 1989, my first year in Kansas City and Christian's third year in the league, he became the AFC Offensive Player of the Year, a phenomenon, and the best football story in a long time.

The Nigerian Nightmare. It was a great nickname because Christian was a sweetheart of a guy. He made the best goat stew I ever tasted. He was easygoing, a people person with an always pleasant demeanor. But then he put a helmet on, and you didn't want to be in his way.

When Coach Schottenheimer and I got to Kansas City, we knew pretty quickly what we had in Christian. Within the first couple days of camp, we timed him in the 40-yard dash, and he clocked a 4.36. It didn't add up that a guy his size could do that, so we made him do it again. He clocked a 4.36 again. That's the way it was all training camp. Christian stood out. He was so big and so fast; we hadn't seen anybody like him. He was raw, of course, but every coach wants the challenge of molding a raw talent into a star.

Christian perfectly fit Schottenheimers's vision for our team. Schottenheimer wanted to run the ball, just as he had so successfully with the Cleveland Browns before coming to Kansas City. He had led the Browns to two AFC Championship Games. Physicality would be our offensive identity, and one look at Christian early in training camp let us know that *Christian* would be our offensive identity.

So, we went to work. The challenge was getting Christian to learn how to channel his tremendous power when he carried the ball. Having power and bringing your power are two different things. He had to learn how to keep his pad level down and enforce himself on people, and there were some drills he worked on to get to where he needed to go. One of them was running into the two-man sled, hitting it with either shoulder, working on ball security, and delivering a blow to the defender. Christian hit that thing over and over, punishing it and driving it backward just like he'd do with opponents. In another drill the runner would get the ball and approach a hole, and either someone from the outside or the inside would emerge to hit you, but you didn't know which one. You had to read it on the move, react, then make a jump cut, and burst through the hole. The key was to run with patience to the hole but then burst through it with explosiveness after the jump cut.

Christian did those drills until their principles were second nature. He'd had a background in track, which is often seen as a knock against football players, but Christian really benefited from the discipline he'd developed in becoming one of the world's best discus throwers. He knew what it felt like to keep working until he got it right and he wouldn't stop until he was satisfied.

That year, 1989, was a watershed year in Kansas City. We drafted Derrick Thomas, Neil Smith came into his own, and our defense emerged as one of the best in the league. Offensively, we had Christian, and, suddenly, after the Chiefs had spent years in the basement, Schottenheimer had brought a winning mentality back to a proud franchise. We narrowly missed the playoffs in '89, but the Chiefs made the playoffs the next six years. I watched it happen before my eyes: the stadium went from half full to having a waitlist for tickets.

None of that would have happened without Christian. There was his talent, of course, but he also had a captivating story. A few short years prior, he had never even seen a football game. All of a sudden, he was one of the best football players in the world.

It was a testament to his amazing athletic talent, sure, but it also said a lot about his work ethic and character. Christian needed a lot of coaching, but he was the definition of coachable. A perfect example of that was on display in a game against the San Francisco 49ers. I'll never forget it. On one play the 49ers forced Christian to cut back, and when he did, Ronnie Lott, one of the hardest-hitting defensive backs in the history of the NFL, blew him up, flattening him. After the play I explained to Christian that this was how the 49ers were playing him. They were making him cut back, and then Lott would come free, and it was up to him to be ready for contact with the future Hall of Famer.

A few plays later, we called the same play, the 49ers did the same thing on defense, and Christian lowered his shoulder and sent Lott in the air. The trainers had to come get Lott. That day Lott learned what we already knew: nobody was more powerful than Christian Okoye, and despite his inexperience, nobody learned faster.

—Bruce Arians
Kansas City Chiefs running backs coach, 1989–92
Arizona Cardinals head coach, 2013–17
Tampa Bay Buccaneers head coach, 2019–21

1

CIVIL WAR

The Nigerian Civil War changed everything about my childhood. It changed everything about my life. It spanned 30 horrific months from 1967 to 1970. At the time people said it was the first televised war, where images of the dead bodies and the starving children were broadcast worldwide. This was Africa. This was the legacy of colonialism.

The death toll was so severe that all we have are estimates: between one million and three million deaths were suffered by the Igbo people—my people. Prior to the war, the Igbo had been persecuted and slaughtered. We tried to break away and start our own country called Biafra, but the Nigerian government wouldn't let us. The civil war was the result.

My family got displaced from our home. We moved to an agricultural compound, and my brothers and I went to school sporadically. We had plenty of time on our hands, and when I was seven, my nine-year-old brother Emmanuel and I decided to visit our oldest brother, Stanislaus. He was about 14, working for a relief agency in another town. Emmanuel and I didn't tell anyone we were leaving. If we had, someone likely would have told us it was a bad idea. Emmanuel and I just set out walking. We walked all day past dusk. But when we showed up at Stan's workplace, we learned he'd been transferred to another city and wasn't around. We were disappointed and turned around to go home to begin the long walk back.

It had been dark for hours by that point—it must have been after midnight—and the road was completely deserted. Finally, we came upon a checkpoint operated by Biafran soldiers. We knew they were Igbo, our people, but they didn't know who we were—and they were hostile and scary. In their minds Emmanuel and I were spies working for the Nigerian government. The soldiers took us to their barracks to interrogate us. We had no idea what to expect or how this was going to end. They asked us if we were with the Nigerian government; they seemed sure we were. We denied it. They asked and asked. We kept denying it. Trying to get us to break, they screamed at us over and over: "You're lying! You're lying!"

I began to get the feeling that we'd never leave those barracks alive. I started to cry. My brother stayed calm. Maybe it was because I was crying, but suddenly the demeanor of the soldiers softened. They believed what we'd been saying all along: we'd merely gone to visit our brother. We weren't enemies. We were children. After that the soldiers became protective of us. They told us it was dangerous out there on those roads. Since we'd spent the previous day walking, we hadn't eaten a meal in about 36 hours, so they fed us. Back then, we were only eating about one meal per day, so we ate voraciously. And when the sun came up and when it was safer on the roads, we spent the next day walking home, grateful to be alive.

When we got home, we saw how relieved our mother was. She and other family members had spent the day looking for us and had been terrified. She asked us where we were, and we told her the whole story, and I remember the look of relief on her face. It was a perilous place to raise kids, and as a father now, I have a better understanding of how nerve-wracking that episode must have been for our parents.

*   *   *

I was born on August 16, 1961, less than a year after my country was granted its independence from the British and I spent the first 21 years of my life in Nigeria. Most American readers have no idea what to picture when they think of Nigeria in the 1960s, so I'll do my best to describe what it was like.

My home city was Enugu, which had been developed by the British as a coal mining center about 45 years before I was born. Its population was about 100,000 when I was a little kid, but now the city has grown to about 800,000 people. It was sort of developed—but sort of not. We didn't live in mud huts, and there weren't animals walking in the streets. The streets were paved, and there were some traffic lights but not as many as you'd see in America, and people didn't always obey them. There weren't any supermarkets, just small storefront markets for this thing or that. We had electricity, but it wasn't consistent like in America. If the electricity went out for days at a time, nobody screamed at the customer service representative on the phone or even batted an eye.

Enugu was the biggest city in the country's southeastern region, which is populated mostly by the Igbo people, one of about 250 ethnolinguistic groups in Nigeria. The country itself is a creation of the British—who we refer to as our "colonial masters"—who mixed these 250 tribes together and called it a country. Nearly everyone I knew was Igbo and practiced Catholicism. The dominant ethnic group in Nigeria, the Hausas, were Muslim and mostly lived in the northern part of the country. In my early childhood, I only knew one Hausa, a friendly man who'd sometimes give us food. When the war came, pitting our ethnicities against each other, he left his home, and I never saw him again.

I grew up in a home with my parents and five other siblings. My father ran a government-run reformatory school. During my early years, we lived on school grounds in a two-bedroom home that was part of a compound built for school staff. But it wasn't the type of two-bedroom place most think of with a garage, a dining room, living room, and den. No, where I come from, a two-bedroom house means the house is just one bedroom, and then another is directly attached to it with a very small, detached kitchen containing just a stove. We shared a yard with seven other families in the compound and shared a bathroom with them as well. There was one toilet and one bath for seven families. It was always in use. We all slept in one room on mats made of interwoven palm leaves. The first time I ever slept in a bed consistently was when I came to Azusa Pacific University at the age of 21.

As for cooking, if we had some extra money, we'd use kerosene, but usually we'd use firewood, meaning that every time we'd want to cook something or boil water, we'd start a fire with the wood. We didn't own a refrigerator because it was too expensive. So anything we ate we cooked and ate on the spot.

Every single morning, the first thing we'd do was walk to the pump to fetch water. The whole family, including the little kids, would go out with the buckets and then come back, carrying the filled buckets on our heads. (We didn't own a vehicle; only the rich people did.) We'd use the water from the buckets to take baths for work or school. Some of the water would be used to cook with, and some of it was our drinking water. We stored it in a clay pot—with a cover on it to keep insects away and to keep it cool—and we'd dip our cup into the pot if we were thirsty.

For entertainment we had one small radio, and that was my first experience of any kind with America. My dad was actually very into country music. He loved Don Williams and Dolly Parton, and I remember him humming country songs around the house. We, though, didn't have a TV. There were a couple of families in our compound who had one, so occasionally we'd go to one of their places and watch mostly American and British movies. We'd see the luxurious houses with manicured lawns or the cities with gleaming tall buildings, new cars, and orderly traffic lights. It was so far-fetched. We had never seen anything like that ever, and those movies just seemed like a complete fantasy for us. It was a pleasant diversion for sure but not something that seemed at all real.

* * *

For years I'd been under the impression that the name *Okoye* means Sunday in the Igbo language, but I recently learned that's not true because there's no such thing as Sunday in the Igbo calendar, where there are four days in a week and *Oye* is the third of the four days. According to my brother Stan, an ancestor of ours was born on *Oye*. If you're a male descendant, according to Igbo custom, you add the prefix *Ok* to your name, which makes *Okoye*. If you're a female, you add the prefix *Nwa*, which would make *Nwaoye*. But that's ancient custom, mostly lost to history. In my immediate family, males and females alike went by *Okoye*.

My dad, Benedict Okoye, was extremely intelligent, but he had never gone to high school because he had to go to work, which cut his potential short. But here's how smart he was: even after he dropped out, his former teachers invited him back to teach at his primary school, even though he was just a teenager. My dad was a man with a very strong sense of right and wrong. He could be stern—he wasn't afraid to spank us, which was the man's job in every Nigerian family I knew—but he had a silly, fun-loving side. I can still picture some of the silly dances he'd do that would make us laugh.

My mom, Cecilia Okoye, had a more serious personality. She was a hard worker who took pride in raising a family that was well-mannered, put together, and, most importantly, well-fed. When we'd go visit people, she made sure we had at least one pair of nice, clean clothes. She had a way of making things work, of hustling. She sold bread out of our house before the war, which she'd buy from wholesalers, and after the war transitioned to selling textiles at the market. She had extraordinary willpower and made things happen.

My parents weren't particularly big people. My mom was tall—5'10" with a medium build—and my father was 5'8" and slim. Looking at them doesn't explain where I got my size. I guess I was just fated to be an American football player—even if I'd never heard of the sport for most of my childhood.

I was the third youngest among my seven siblings. We each had our roles within the family. Benedeth, my sister and the oldest of all of us, was the responsible one. Stan, my oldest brother, was the guy who knew all the angles and seemed to know everyone in town. Loretta, the next oldest, was the quiet one who was smarter than all of us. Emmanuel, two years older than I, was the technical one who could take apart a radio and put it back together just to see how it works. My younger brother, Chikwelu, was the organized, particular one. And my younger sister, Obiageli, was the wise, empathic, caring one.

And me? I was the jokester. High energy, always running around playing sports, always getting up to something. I'd make my siblings laugh, and seeing their reactions would make me want to make them laugh some more.

I'd do crazy stuff, just to push things. I'd chase down a chicken, grab it by the neck, and choke it a little bit. I'd stick my hand in a fire and see how long I could leave it in for. Anything for a laugh, anything for some reaction.

Some of us went by English names, and some of us went by Igbo names. That's the way it was in our house. We spoke a mix of English and Igbo with words from either language mixed in here and there. Igbo was our first language, but we learned English in school, and my dad was comfortable in English, so he spoke it about 70 percent around the house. I'm fluent in both. When I talk to my siblings, I mostly speak Igbo, sprinkling in some English words. This was symbolic of my upbringing, which was a mixture of Western and traditional influences. At the homes of a couple of families in my compound, we watched westerns—*A Fistful of Dollars, The Good, the Bad and the Ugly*—and collected cards from those Clint Eastwood movies that came with chewing gum. We'd go to the nearby bushes and play Cowboys and Indians. We listened to our small radio, and I became a huge Parton fan like my dad. My favorite song is "Coat of Many Colors" about a mom who makes a beautiful coat by sewing together a bunch of rags. It was a similar magic to the way our parents, even though we were poor, always made us feel like we didn't need anything more.

So we had those American traditions, but we valued our Igbo traditions as well, especially the food. Nigerians are just like any group: we show love through food. Food becomes even more important if it's scarce. In my early childhood before the war, I never went hungry, but there was never anything extra. We enjoyed what we had, including jollof rice with a tomato base and flavored with curry powder; okra soup with the gooeyness of the okra giving it some heft and whatever meats you had thrown into the pot adding different flavors; and bitter leaf soup, where the leaf must be rinsed out several times to take out the bitterness. When it's done right, it is savory and robust. We also had egusi soup made of ground melon seeds, which gives a nutty flavor. Our recipes require patience and mastery of techniques that are passed down through generations. Everything we eat in Nigeria has a deep, bold flavor. We don't hold back on spices. When I came to Kansas City and had really good barbecue for the first time, it was actually quite similar.

Another Igbo tradition is the masquerades, where our ancient religious traditions are channeled and the tangible world meets the spiritual world. As a kid during holiday season, a group of us would roam around town watching the masquerades and the incredible costumes the performers wore. Masks carved of wood represented the whole gamut of emotions and spirits, outfits were made of dried palm leaves, and the performers danced and did unbelievably acrobatic things. The masquerades would move around town, as the drumbeat heralded their arrival with different traditional instruments signaling the type of spirits—sometimes benevolent, sometimes evil—they represented. The music would be so hypnotic and the dancing would be so spectacular that it felt like you were in a trance.

Sometimes we'd just watch, but many of the masquerades were more interactive with more aggressive spirits, and the performers would chase the kids who walked past them. If you got caught, you'd get flogged with a cane. They didn't flog you too hard, but it hurt enough so that running away from them with your friends gave us a feeling of danger and thrill. That was some of the most fun I've ever had. The masquerades would only happen a few times a year: Christmas, Easter, New Year's, and in August for the harvesting of yams for the New Yam Festival or *Ji Ofu* in the Igbo language. For almost the whole year, we lived basically Western lives, but the holidays were a time to celebrate our own traditions. We were Igbo and we were a unique and proud people.

So that was my early childhood. Our family was loving, and we had a lot of fun. I describe us as being poor, but we didn't know it. Besides, in a place like Nigeria, "poor" is a relative term. When I picture my early childhood, I picture myself playing and laughing.

And then civil war broke out.

*   *   *

I was five years old when the war started. This means I knew nothing about the tensions between the Igbos and the Hausas. I had no idea the Hausas were the dominant group who controlled the government and military and that the Igbo were second-class citizens. I knew nothing about colonialism or the fact that Nigeria only became an independent country the year before I was born. I knew nothing about Nigeria's first ever elections after becoming a republic in 1964, which were marred by fraud and allowed the Hausas to cement their power. I knew nothing about the coup launched by Igbo military men in response—or the countercoup the Hausas launched a few months later.

I knew nothing about the persecution the Hausas rained down on the Igbos after that. Somewhere between 10,000 and 30,000 Igbo people—civilians—were killed before the war even started. There were brutal pogroms, where a group of guys would come into a home, beat up the men, and rape the women. I knew nothing about the Igbo's attempt to secede and create our own country, the Republic of Biafra, which led to the civil war. I didn't know the British threw their support behind the Nigerian government—and against us—arming the soldiers who were killing my people. The West wanted to keep borders exactly where they'd decided they should be. I had no idea that the United States by staying neutral was tacitly siding with the British.

My older siblings would sometimes listen to news of the war on the radio, but I had no idea that images of the horror were being broadcast throughout the world. Because of a blockade of humanitarian supplies imposed by the Nigerian government, famine took hold. Most of the millions of Igbo deaths during the war came from starvation, not combat.

Though the war ended when I was eight, I was only vaguely aware at the time that our side had lost and that the dream of an independent Igbo country was not to be. As a result, for the duration of my childhood and continuing to the present day, to be an Igbo in Nigeria meant to be a marginalized minority. No, I wasn't fully aware of any of that, but there were some things I did know.

I knew I was walking with my brother Emmanuel to school when we saw a dead body on the side of the road. Curiosity drew us to it. When we got close, we saw it was an Igbo soldier. We saw several others throughout the war, hoping the next body wasn't one of our uncles who'd gone off to fight for our side. If you've never seen war up close, count your blessings. You never fully escape a moment like that. A part of me will always be that six year old who came upon that dead body.

I knew what *kwashiorkor* was. That is the malnutrition that causes the bellies of kids to swell and protrude. I used to talk about it with my friends. I'd see those kids with those bellies and knew some of them. I knew I was a couple of bad breaks away from being one of them. I knew that in late 1967 my family needed to leave our home. The war front had moved to Enugu as the Nigerian government forces moved in to take the city. (They would do so in short order.) Word got around quickly that it was no longer safe. So our first move was to flag down a truck to get to Agukwu Nri, a town about two hours away, where we had extended family.

But that didn't last long because soon we saw shells exploding overhead, which meant the war was coming closer and we had no time to waste. We gathered whatever belongings we could and walked along a long road to an agricultural compound we'd heard was safe in a town called Adazi, which was a few miles away.

To a little kid like me, carrying all that stuff made the walk seem like it lasted forever. I remember being incredibly hungry, a feeling I'd get used to over the next two years. But the feeling I remember most is being relieved that we were getting away from danger. I'm not sure I even registered the danger itself—only that I was happy to be getting away from it. On the walk, as hungry as I was, I remember thinking to myself, *All I can do is be patient and keep going.* So I did. When I think back about how the war helped form my personality, I think of that walk.

The agricultural compound was basically a big warehouse that had been used to store chickens before they were slaughtered. In other words, it was not fit for human habitation. It was a huge empty space with no walls. So we got there and put our stuff down in one corner of the building. Several other families did the same. At the time I was under the impression that we'd be there for a few weeks until the danger passed either at our home in Enugu or with extended family in Agukwu Nri. We stayed for about two years.

There was a school, which is one reason why my parents sought out that place, though with everything going on, none of us children went consistently. My parents' primary focus was securing food, and thanks to them, we usually had it, though not much of it. We'd usually eat once a day mostly in the late afternoon. My father by this point was working for the Biafran government, so he'd send food items like rice, beans, and yams, often flagging down a truck and sending the food on the truck because those are the types of trust and bonds you see where I come from despite the horror that was going on everywhere. My mom hustled, always working, making deals, and scrounging up food. I admired both my parents so much. Even though I was a small child, I didn't take any of this for granted. Every day the food would appear. Every time I was grateful for my parents and proud of them.

What's strange is that as messed up as everything was and with all the horror taking place around us, I don't remember being unhappy during that time period. Mostly, I played. We had no toys, but we had fun. We'd play in a nearby bush, chasing birds around or maybe throwing rocks at them. We'd grab some old rags, tie them together to make a makeshift ball, and play soccer. It was a lesson to me that in life you make do with what you have.

*   *   *

Eventually, the war ended. I don't remember being told the war was over, but I do remember my mom telling us that we finally could leave the agricultural compound. I was nine years old by then and I felt relief. But the war had changed a lot of things for the worse. I'd hear the stories from other kids that someone's father or uncle went off to war and never came home.

My hometown, Enugu, had been devastated. Since it was the capital of Biafra, it was captured by the government forces and shelled out. Stores were looted, and everyone fled, including employers. Just because the war was now over didn't mean the economy and people's lives went back to normal.

Enugu had been occupied by the Nigerian government forces and subjected to horrific brutality. Ruthlessness was part of the war strategy. I recently saw an article from *The New York Times* that quoted an order given to Nigerian soldiers: "You are therefore required to push ahead ruthlessly to vanquish the rebels in your way," the order read. "You will tell this to all your men because rebels have no honor and no respect for the dignity of mankind."

I'd overhear the adults talking about this ruthlessness—the raping and murdering of men, women, and children for its own sake. All of it seemed abstract, too horrible to even wrap my head around or even believe. Now that I'm older, I believe every one of those stories.

Initially, I thought we'd go back home, but that never happened. We lost our old place on the school grounds because the school had closed during the war and didn't reopen. This meant we were out of a home, and my father was out of a job. We wound up moving into a place my grandfather owned in a part of town called Coal Camp, which used to house the coal miners back when Enugu was a coal mining center. It was a major step down. Everything was older and a lot more cramped. We knew we had moved into the ghetto. Our financial situation also wasn't good. We were eating better than we were during the war but not nearly as well as we'd had been before it started. Things weren't back to normal by any stretch.

One big reason for why we had so little was a particular measure taken by the Nigerian government. During the war the government changed the currency, and it declared bank accounts owned by Igbos as worthless. After the war ended, they gave Igbos, who had bank accounts, a measly 20 pounds, which is all my family was left with. We never had a lot of savings, but we had more than 20 pounds. Basically, we had to start from scratch. My dad tried to find another job after his school closed, but with the economy in tatters, he couldn't get work for two years. We could sense his stress around the house, and it was heartbreaking because we knew how smart, devoted, and capable he was.

With my dad not bringing any income in, my mom had to pick up the slack. She switched from selling bread out of our home to selling textiles at the market. It gave me so much respect for her to see how tireless she was, but every morning I'd also see how worried she was, and that made me sad. There was just so much pressure on her every day to hustle up enough money to feed her family.

But that was life for us and millions of other Igbo people. For most of us, there weren't any good opportunities. Every good government job went to the Hausas. The vast majority of the military was Hausa. Even more than before the war, we were segregated in the southeastern part of the country, where there were no Hausa people in sight. We knew we were being ruled by a distant power hundreds of miles away. We'd lost the war and had to accept that we were in Nigeria, but it didn't feel like our country. The freezing of our bank accounts itself sent that message: our money was no longer good here.

I'm sure there are stereotypes about Igbos, just like there are stereotypes of any marginalized group. But I never heard any of them; it's not like I internalized any feelings of inferiority. My take has always been that bullies don't need a reason to bully people. That was more than 50 years ago, and though things have improved since then, the basic problem is still the same: the Igbos are the underclass, and the Hausas are the ruling class. In the 1950s huge amounts of oil were discovered in the country, mostly on Igbo land. Yet, foreign companies and the Hausa elite mostly control the supply, and the Igbos don't benefit. To this day, virtually no high-ranking government or military officials are Igbos.

Because of this there's a new movement among Igbos who are pushing for a Biafran state again. Their approach is belligerent; they'll bully and terrorize other Igbos who don't support their militant stance. Almost all of them are young, which makes sense because if they were old enough to experience the war they would want no part of it. These people are playing with fire and they don't even know it.

After the civil war, we knew that more bloodshed wasn't the answer. But what was? We didn't know. We looked around at the devastation of our surroundings. Then, on TV and radio, we'd see images of America and Britain. They looked like advanced societies with easy luxury and lifestyles of plenty. As a kid, I didn't fully understand everything that was happening, but the older I got, the more I began to realize that if I wanted to make something of myself, I needed to get out of Nigeria.

2

SOCCER DREAMS

My memories of my teenage years mainly consist of two things: playing sports and spending time with my mom. Starting when I was about 11, I became my mom's primary helper around the house because my oldest siblings went off to boarding school, making me the oldest kid still at home. American readers might get the wrong impression, thinking that my siblings going to boarding school is an indication we had money. But in Nigeria going away for school doesn't cost nearly as much money, and my family scraped together whatever we could, including borrowing from relatives. It shows how much emphasis my family—and my culture in general—placed on education.

What it meant for me was that I was with my mom a lot—something I was grateful for at the time and became even more grateful for a few years later, when my mom passed away. I was 16.

I admired her deeply. I remember her face when she woke up every morning. She always had a serious look in her eye and an expression of worry. Especially in those first few years after the war when my dad was out of a job, every morning the question needed to be answered: *How will I feed my family today?*

Everything in her life revolved around that question. And yet she was warm and open-hearted. She taught me many things, but the most important lesson was that you should trust people until they prove they can't be trusted. Greet strangers with a smile. Assume they're good people. Sometimes they'll disappoint you but usually not.

She also taught me to cook, including how to make the egusi soup and the okra soup that I make to this day, and every time I do, the smell reminds me of her. She taught me how to help her out when she went to the market to sell the textiles called *abada*, which she got wholesale. I loved going with her and seeing the way she went about her business. My mom was exactly what a businesswoman should be. She had loyal customers because she was loyal to them. They knew she was fair, that she wasn't trying to gouge them, and that the quality of the garments she sold was always top-notch. Nigeria is that kind of place. Your reputation is everything, and word of mouth gets around to everyone. My mom was respected and beloved. Her customers would come and stay for hours, just chatting with her, and she'd send me out to buy a soft drink for them. I was proud to be my mom's son.

One incident I remember vividly sums up my mom perfectly. We were at a market stall, where she had to peddle her wares, but my mom had to leave for a few minutes, so I was there alone. A woman came in and started asking to see the garments, but she left without buying anything. I knew our inventory by heart, so that after she left, I realized quickly that something was missing. The woman must have been a professional thief who'd distracted me by making me fetch an item while she stuffed something in her bag.

I was nervous my mom would be angry with me when she got back. And it's true; she was furious. But not at me. She couldn't get over the idea that this woman had taken advantage of a kid. It went against everything that she stood for, and what she stood for was good values. She'd lived through a civil war that had killed millions of her own people, and even after that, a woman stealing something under the nose of a child bothered her on a profound level.

I admired her so much and I saw how much she did for us. So one day, when I was about 12, I decided I wanted to do something nice for her. I decided to take her to the zoo. At the time my oldest sister, Benedeth, was a police officer making decent money, so my plan was to ask Benedeth for money for a cab and admission. Benedeth gave me what I asked for, and I remember how proud I was when I walked up to my mother and said, "Mom, get ready. I'm taking you to the zoo."

But when we got to the gate to buy tickets, it turned out I didn't have enough money. I'd had no idea how much it would cost and I hadn't asked Benedeth for enough. But it was okay because my mom made up the difference, and then we spent one of the best days of my life together at that Enugu Zoo, looking at the giraffes, the elephants, the antelopes, the lions. I could see how happy my mom was and how being around the animals took her away from all of her worries. I could see how touched she was by the gesture. For weeks afterward she'd tell her friends: "Christian took me to the zoo." It made me so proud.

She started getting sick early on in those years. She'd get dizzy a lot; she'd get headaches that would never quit. It was high blood pressure, which runs in our family. Still, she carried on, hustling all the time, which I'm sure made her condition worse. At a certain point, she went to the doctor. This was the 1970s in an impoverished part of Nigeria, so the doctor didn't tell her to change her diet. Instead he prescribed medication, but the dose he gave was way more than she needed, and she wound up getting ever sicker from the meds. So at the behest of my dad, she stopped taking them. She felt better temporarily, but it didn't change the overall picture: her blood pressure was too high, and nobody knew what to do about it.

When she had the massive stroke that killed her, she was just 55. For the 10 days she stayed alive after her stroke, she laid in her hospital bed awake but looked like she was asleep because she physically couldn't open her eyes. The pain I felt about seeing her in that condition has stuck with me ever since. The mom I knew was so vivacious, so on top of everything. I rubbed her hand and rubbed her face. My thought was that when she returned to normal I would tell her about all the people who visited her and what she missed, and we'd go on like we had before.

When she died I was shocked—too shocked to even process the reality that she was gone. I didn't cry at the time and I didn't cry for years afterward because for years it didn't even seem real. The first time I remember crying was when I left to go to America and I'd think about her and how proud she'd be that I was going to college overseas. I'd sit in my college dorm room at Azusa Pacific and sob. She worked so hard for us to have a better future, and here I was living in that better future. That's when it hit me that she was gone.

*   *   *

Before my mom died, my days followed a pattern. I'd go to school and then I'd come home and do my chores. Then I'd go out and play soccer with my friends until way past dark—way past when I was supposed to. Playing soccer was the only thing I ever wanted to do. Back then, we had cricket and basketball, which we called "Netball," as well in Nigeria, but for me nothing compared to soccer. My friends and I were pretty straightlaced.

Nobody I knew was into stealing stuff, damaging property, taking drugs or even alcohol. All we wanted to do was hang out and play sports with each other.

The one thing I never did? Study. It wasn't that I wasn't intellectually curious. I loved history because it was about people and how they're different but really all the same and I enjoyed the Bible classes we take in Nigeria because I've always been serious about my faith and I enjoyed the stories. But as a kid, I didn't have the patience or attention span to sit down and do schoolwork. So I never did. And that pissed off my dad.

My dad was an exceptionally smart man whose potential was cut short because he'd had to leave school early and then, of course, his career was derailed because of the war. It took him two-and-a-half years to find work after the war; he eventually found a job as a store manager, which was way beneath his level of intellect. Like so many Nigerian parents, he knew education was the path to success, and nothing was more important to him as a parent than making sure his kids were educated.

I'm not sure people fully appreciate how much value Nigerians place on education. It's *everything*, and you see that now with Nigerian Americans, who are one of this country's most successful immigrant groups. About 60 percent of Nigerian Americans have at least a bachelor's degree—about double that of the American population—and 29 percent have graduate degrees compared to 11 percent of the American population, according to the Migrations Policy Institute.

In post-civil war Nigeria, if you were an Igbo, it was hard to find much hope for achieving success. But one thing was certain: if you didn't have an education, you had zero chance. So when my dad saw me playing soccer at all hours and frittering away my future, he wouldn't stand for it. It's not like my dad was a stern, no-fun guy who had no use for games; the opposite is true. He had a silly sense of humor and loved music and life and, in his youth, he'd even been an excellent soccer player in his youth. But he'd sustained a bunch of injuries playing soccer and had to stop playing anyway because of his many responsibilities, and that put things in perspective for him: soccer was fun but not important. My dad wasn't about to watch his son ruin his chances of succeeding because of a game.

So what did my dad do when I continually defied him and played soccer, neglecting my studies? He whooped my ass—literally—with a cane. In my memory this happened practically every day for several years in my youth. The pattern went like this: he'd tell me he'd want me home at a certain time, and I'd nod and say yes, but, of course, I'd stay out playing, and my dad would come find me. Then he'd take me home, take out the cane, tell me in a calm voice exactly what I did wrong, and take a cane to my bare ass.

Some readers might take away from this that my dad was this intimidating, angry guy. That's not at all what he was like. If you don't understand our culture, it's hard to picture it, but there was a way to discipline kids, and it was every father's job to administer the discipline. So that's what my dad did. I never once felt that my father was being abusive. I never thought: *Screw this guy* and defied him just to spite him. No, I knew what he was telling me was right and I respected him. But when I was playing soccer, I'd think to myself, *Just 10 more minutes…* And then 10 minutes would turn into a half hour, and then a half hour would turn into two hours.

One time I was playing goalie in a game, looking out onto the action on the field, and I noticed everyone had stopped playing. I wondered what had happened, but then I turned around and saw my dad behind me, and thought to myself, *Ohhh, shit.* I'd often see my dad coming from far away down the street and, thinking he hadn't seen me, I'd run into the bushes to hide. But I never got away with it. Several times I'd take a bucket to the field because I'd fetch water for my family on the way back and, after I'd hidden, I'd come back onto the field and notice the bucket was missing. It was my dad's way of telling me he knew all my tricks and I couldn't get away with anything.

My dad wasn't a big guy, but I was obviously getting bigger and bigger. But I never once thought about fighting back against him when he was disciplining me. In Nigeria that's simply out of the realm of possibility. Had I done that, my older brothers would've kicked my ass. Other relatives would have, too. If a stranger on the street would have seen a younger person fighting back against an older person, the stranger would've kicked my ass, too.

So it went in my childhood. I wasn't the easiest son for my dad to have. But I never doubted he loved me, and he never doubted I loved and respected him.

Soccer was the perfect sport for me for many reasons. First of all, I had a never-ending supply of energy, and in soccer you're running all the time. I also grew up in a small house in a cramped neighborhood, so I loved running in a wide-open space. Also, I was a social kid, who loved being around his friends, and soccer at its heart is a social sport. It's all about teamwork, being creative alongside other people, and your intuition of what other people are doing and thinking.

I couldn't get enough soccer—both playing it and following it as a fan. If there was a big professional game, whether for teams in Nigeria or the big European leagues, I'd try to find a TV to watch it, usually standing in the doorway of a neighbor's house. I studied photos and videos of Pele and, more locally, the star player on the local Enugu team named Christian

Chuku. He was my favorite player and he went on to become the captain of the national team. I felt a special connection to him because his name was Christian.

We were too poor to ever attend a pro game, but I'd read the newspapers and the magazines, and the players became larger than life, growing in stature in my mind because I could never see them play live. I loved how different players had different styles. I loved the brilliant, acrobatic ways they scored goals.

Playing soccer professionally was my dream, and in that way, I was no different from the millions of kids across the globe who grow up in poverty and dream of soccer as their ticket to a better future. But when I say "dream," I mean it was literally my dream. Throughout my whole childhood, I had a recurring dream where it would actually rain soccer balls from the sky. Millions of soccer balls would come down from the heavens. I had this dream for years because it contained everything that I ever wanted. In real life my family could never afford a soccer ball and I never owned one. In this dream I had more soccer balls than I could ever want, and the whole world was soccer, soccer, soccer.

But when I entered my teenage years, I got bigger. I grew and grew—and kept growing. By the age of 14, I was about 5'11" and approaching 200 pounds. In sports getting big is usually a good thing, but soccer is an exception. It's no coincidence that short guys like Pele, Lionel Messi, and Diego Maradona are three of the best players of all time. In soccer being built low to the ground gives you an advantage in controlling the ball. When I was 14, I was too big, too hulking. Despite my love for the sport, I just wasn't as good as a lot of smaller kids and I knew I couldn't play the sport at the high school level.

But still I had my energy, which meant I needed a sport to play. It so happened that my best friend, Adolphus Onua, started running track—the hurdles specifically—and he loved it, so I decided to join him on the track team. Soon, I got too big for the hurdles and switched to shot put, discus, and the hammer throw. I was a natural at those sports and loved them immediately. That's a quality of mine I think I got from my mom. I'm very open to new experiences and I'm always moving forward, trying to make the best of situations.

The discus, in particular, I loved. Most people don't appreciate all the technique that goes into it, but to be a good discus thrower means that countless body parts have to be in perfect harmony. To have a good heave with the spin coming off your fingertips at just the right angle to get the perfect glide is a beautiful and satisfying thing. It's like hitting a good golf shot or a home run in baseball, where you get it just right, and the distance it travels almost surprises you. That's what your body can do when everything's in sync.

So, I was having a good time doing track and I was good at it. But my track career probably would have ended in high school had Onua not made the state team, where he was coached by a man named Patrick Anukwa. Onua told me Anukwa was an outstanding coach who had gotten the best out of him—and he wanted to meet me. It was a meeting that changed my life.

*   *   *

Patrick Anukwa was a lot like my father. He was calm and direct with a way of saying things that made them very clear. He was one of those people who seemed like he was born to be a coach. He'd been sent by the Nigerian government to America to a coaching academy where he'd learned the most advanced methods of coaching track. After he returned he became the coach for Anambra State, which at the time included my hometown of Enugu. It was obvious that he knew things that a lot of other people didn't.

When I met Anukwa, he saw how big and strong I was and also that I was coordinated. He knew quickly that my best event would be discus, which involves more technique than shot put, and he told me that if I worked at it, discus could get me pretty far. But first he needed to convince my father that this would be a good thing for me.

He met my father face to face as a gesture of respect. He told him that he would personally bring me home after practice every day in time for me to do my homework. He told him he would personally see to it that I'd do my schoolwork and become a serious student because if I didn't, then I couldn't train with him. My dad saw that Coach Anukwa was sincere and wanted what was best for me. He agreed to let me join the team.

I was excited and, with Anukwa's encouragement about my potential in track, I became very focused. All the frenetic energy I'd always had inside me was now channeled into one goal: becoming the best discus thrower I could be. I was going to represent my school and—because of Anukwa—my entire state as well.

I worked hard and immediately saw the results in my discus marks. It became a positive feedback loop. Seeing my improvement made me hungry for even better marks, so I worked harder and got even better results. So I worked even harder, and on and on it went. On the state team, we traveled all around Nigeria and stayed in hotels. That was a big deal for me. After I'd spent every night of my life sleeping on mats woven out of palm leaves, suddenly I was sleeping in a bed! In a hotel! In my own room! It was one of many signs that with track and field I was on a good path. Maybe the only path. After I graduated high school,

I had no idea what I'd do with myself. Getting a job didn't really appeal to me, but my athletic talent bailed me out. In Nigeria at the time, various companies fielded competitive teams in various sports, and the national telephone company was putting together a track team and wanted me to be a part of it. I was given a job at the telephone company, but it was a no-show job. The only real work I had to do was to train for their track competitions and compete for their company team.

I was 18 and had no idea what I wanted to do with my life. But I liked sports and I liked getting paid, so this job with the power company was a good thing. Track had gotten me to this point. I had no idea how much further it would get me.

3

MAN ON A MISSION

I graduated from high school in 1979. I came to Azusa Pacific University in California in the summer of 1982. In between was a dizzying series of events and good fortune.

The first was being selected for the Nigerian national camp for track. I was already on the Enugu state team training with Patrick Anukwa, but being on the national team brought another level of prestige. About twice a year, we'd go to weeks-long camps to train with athletes from other parts of Nigeria. The competition brought out the best in all of us. And we had tons of fun.

It was a mixture of guys from all backgrounds—Igbo, Hausa, Yoruba, some of the many other tribes that make up Nigeria—and for the first time in my life, I made friends with people from different ethnicities. I'd hear all different languages around the camp, but when we'd all sit down for meals together or talk on the field, we'd speak English—or what used to be called "Broken English"—and everyone got along great. That's an image that has stuck in my mind: a bunch of guys from different tribes eating egusi soup and fufu and cracking jokes, having the best time.

The war had ended just 10 years before, but among us it was as if it had never happened. We were a team and we were proud to represent Nigeria. It goes to show that wars are between governments—not people as individuals—and that there's no reason for war because on an individual level almost every person is decent, and people will get along. That was a great lesson to me, one that has made me a better person.

I also became a better athlete during these camps. Often, I'd challenge the sprinters to races. My legs were powerful, and I had very good acceleration, but once it got to about 30 meters, I couldn't keep up with them. The sprinters' turnover—or the rate at which their feet touched the ground—was just much better than mine, and once they got into their strides, they'd leave me in the dust. But I kept challenging them and picked their brains about how they trained to improve their turnovers or get out of the blocks quickly. I couldn't help myself; it was my high-energy nature. I was approaching 20, but I was the same kid who'd always wanted to run around and play soccer at all hours.

Even though I was training for discus and shot put, I got a lot faster during those years. I learned how to listen to my body to improve subtle things, like acceleration and speed, that people assume is natural and can't be improved upon with technique. I didn't know it at the time, but on those track fields in Nigeria, I was training to be an NFL running back.

*   *   *

One of those sprinters I'd challenge to races was a kid from Enugu named Innocent Egbunike. He was about 5'10" but had the legs of a guy who was 6'3". From the side it looked like his hip was about halfway up his torso, which gave him a long stride that enabled him to take over races once he got going. Egbunike ran like a gazelle and was the best athlete out of all of us in those camps and in 1980 he was selected for the Nigerian Olympic team that went to Moscow.

We'd been on the Enugu state team together and became close off the bat. Egbunike was my kind of guy: solid values, down to earth, close to his family, and serious about getting better at track. At the same time, he was happy-go-lucky—not a jokester himself but someone who loved to laugh. After the Olympics Egbunike got on the radar of American colleges. He had multiple offers from big-name schools, but the one he was interested in was a small school in California that hardly anybody in America had ever heard of—let alone in Nigeria—called Azusa Pacific University. An Evangelical Christian school about 30 miles west of downtown Los Angeles and nestled in the San Gabriel Valley, Azusa didn't even compete in the NCAA; it was an NAIA school.

Why Azusa? It was simple. Egbunike's mom, like all Nigerian mothers, was overjoyed about the prospect of her son coming to America to get an education. But with the images of American pop culture beamed into Nigerian households—images of sex, violence, and decadence—she was also terrified and was convinced that Egbunike would become a womanizer or a drug addict if he went to a mainstream state school. So Egbunike and his family went looking for Christian schools, preferably near Los Angeles, the site of the 1984 Olympics. One of our friends' fathers happened to be a pastor who'd learned of Azusa through a conference in America he'd gone to. And just like that, this obscure NAIA school got an Olympic athlete, whose record in the 400 meters is still the school's best to this day. As for me, though I had no idea at the time, I'd gotten my foothold into America and the athletic career that would change my life.

Egbunike left for Azusa in the summer of 1981. He wasn't the first person I knew to go to America, but he was my first friend to go. The night before his flight overseas, we had a big going-away party for him. I was excited for his sake and also because Egbunike's going to America made that hope seem tangible for me.

I went with Egbunike and his family to the airport before he flew to America. I'd asked him to put a word in for me with Azusa's track coach, Terry Franson, though I didn't really think much would come of that. But at the airport just before I said good-bye to him, Egbunike looked me in the eye. "I'll get you to America," he said.

A few months later, Egbunike was off doing his thing at Azusa, and I was back home in Enugu with my dad and my siblings, training as hard as ever but not thinking so much about America. I still had hope, and that hope motivated my training, but I was a realist, too, and the reality was most people never made it out, no matter how talented. That's the reality for people living in poverty in every corner of the globe.

Then, one day when I got home from school, I got an envelope at my house—with a stamped letterhead from Azusa Pacific University in California. I opened it up and saw a letter from Franson, the track coach. He wrote that Egbunike had told him all about me—that I was great in the discus, shot put, and hammer and that I was a hard worker. The envelope contained a school admission form, which I filled out. I sent my marks, my transcript, and as a bonus, some newspaper clippings and a photo of myself.

The surge of emotion that went through my body when I got that letter is impossible to describe. You have to understand: when you grow up in Nigeria, where the vast majority of people have never been on an airplane before, there's a special status given to those who have been abroad, especially to America. To us, America was just a fantasy where everything was just *better*—roads, vehicles, cars, everything. That applied to athletics as well. Our state team coach, Patrick Anukwa, had benefited from going to America, and because he had, we all revered him as someone to listen to. Guys who'd been to America for school would come back and regale us with stories about the better facilities, better nutrition, better training.

Now, with that one letter, I was set to be one of those guys. The letter was in my hands, and once I had absorbed what it said, I started jumping up and down. But then I showed my dad, and he was skeptical. He pointed out that there were a lot of steps between getting that letter from Coach Franson and setting foot in the United States. There were a lot of things that could go wrong.

My dad's life experience had taught him that hope often turns into disappointment. This was the same guy who was at the head of his class in school and then had to quit school. The same guy who ran a reformatory school, inspiring countless students and turning around countless lives, only to find himself out of a job for years because of circumstances beyond his control. He always wanted what was best for us and had worked hard to raise us the right way, but his learned instinct was to hedge against disappointment. He told me to temper my hopes. Nothing was confirmed yet, so it wasn't time to celebrate.

But then several weeks later, I got something else in the mail: an I-20 form from the United States government, certifying that I was enrolled in a program to study in America. It was official, and I was ecstatic. My dad was, too, but even then he had reservations. My scholarship from Azusa provided tuition, but there were a lot of other things that cost money like room and board. My dad wondered who would pay the rest of my expenses.

When I think back on his reaction, I think a part of him was still hedging against disappointment. Another part of him, I think, was teaching me that even when things are going great, there are always practical matters to address, and that part of growing up is keeping these practical matters in mind. But I had kept them in mind—and I had answers for my dad. Egbunike was in the exact same financial situation I was and he'd been working jobs on campus to pay his room and board like custodial duties and doing some light construction. He'd told me he could get me the same jobs, so I told my dad, "I'm gonna make this happen."

I think it then clicked for my dad how determined I was. He was proud of me, and I was proud of myself because he was proud of me. Still, I think he had some mixed feelings. To imagine his son 8,000 miles away in America made him anxious. My dad was a very savvy, knowledgeable man, but he'd never been to America and had no idea what that would be like. He wouldn't be able to talk to me about the pitfalls of America. And if anything happened to me, he was an ocean and a continent away. He was excited about my adventure, but he had some fear of the unknown.

After getting the I-20, I still needed to get my travel visa and passport. I'd have to go to the American consulate in Lagos about 350 miles away. I'd gotten the I-20 a couple of months before I was due in school, but I wanted to get those other documents in my hand as soon as possible. The way I thought about it: to hesitate at all was to tempt fate.

My older brother, Stanislaus, the one who'd worked for a relief organization during the war, was by then a taxi driver, so he offered to take a day off work to drive me to Lagos. We set off driving along the highway, but about an hour away from Enugu on the way to Lagos while passing by a market, a car crossed right in front of us. I don't know if the guy was trying to get to the other side of the highway or what, but we couldn't stop in time and we T-boned that car. Because wearing a seatbelt just wasn't something we did in those days, I went flying into the windshield, smacking my head against it and shattering the window. Nobody was badly hurt, thank God, but I was dazed. I stepped out of the car gingerly, and glass was everywhere—all over my clothes and on the ground like a bomb had gone off. My brother's car was totaled.

While we were standing around assessing everything, my brother, by complete chance, saw a friend of his who was going back to Enugu. I was the only one who was even slightly injured, so my brother asked his friend to take me back home. I'd shattered the windshield with my head after all, so the plan was for me to go home to check in with my dad and rest up.

It seemed clear that Lagos, the visa, and passport weren't happening that day. And on the drive back to Enugu, I remember feeling extremely disappointed. I *needed* to get to Lagos. It wasn't rational, but I was afraid that if this sequence of events, starting with Egbunike going to America, paused at all, that it might stop completely, and I'd be stuck in Nigeria for the rest of my life. But just then I remembered I still hadn't collected my latest paycheck from the power company. With that realization came the hope that this could happen that day after all.

Sitting in that car, I hatched a plan. I would grab that paycheck, then I'd use the money to catch a flight from Enugu to Lagos, where my sister, Benedeth, lived. Then I'd find my way to the embassy. I didn't tell my brother's friend because he would've yelled at me that I was being reckless and told me I needed to go home. Instead, I just asked him to drop me off at a bus stop, saying I'd take a bus and get home myself. He did what I asked.

But instead of going home, I took the bus to the power company office and grabbed my paycheck. Then I took a cab to the airport—I'd been there once before to see Egbunike off—and bought a ticket to Lagos. Before I knew it, I was sitting on an airplane for the first time in my life. It all felt like a dream. Nothing about that day seemed real. A few times I had to close my eyes and then open them just to confirm I was awake. I was on a mission. It felt like God was pushing me along, saying, "Get yourself to Lagos, and everything will be okay."

The plane touched down in Lagos; it was the early evening by this point. I had enough money from my paycheck for a cab to Benedeth's house. Benedeth had been a police officer, but she'd retired after having five kids and she was home when I rang the doorbell. She was extremely surprised to see me. "What's going on?" she asked.

I told her the whole story.

Benedeth arranged for me to stay that night in Lagos at the house of another relative named Silvester Ayika, and I woke up early the next morning to go to the embassy. I wanted to get there super early to beat the crowds because there were a lot of people in Nigeria who were desperate like me to get to America. The American officials at the embassy sat me down for a short interview, which was a surreal experience in itself. I'd seen movies, so I knew how Americans talked, but here I was face to face with them—*actual Americans*. After the interview they asked me to sit down. Forty-five minutes went by, and they called my name. A guy handed me a passport and visa and said, "Congratulations."

I had a powerful urge to jump up and down right there in the middle of the embassy, but I kept that excitement within. I took a bus back to Enugu, and the whole time, my body felt like something inside me was jumping up and down. It felt impossible to contain my excitement. It felt amazing.

The first thing I did was to go straight to my dad's office. I figured by then he would have heard about the car crash, which had been not much longer than 24 hours prior. I thought he'd be mad at me for being so reckless. I told him: "Dad, I got the visa."

His face broke into a huge smile. Then he started laughing hard. He said, "I knew it! I knew you'd do it!" And he kept laughing.

I think back to that moment as a father myself and I can relate to my dad's joy. I told him about the crazy journey of the past day and I could see how proud he was. Throughout my childhood he'd tried hard to keep me in line, and as a hard-headed kid with a mind of his own, I'd always pushed back on him. But all he ever wanted was what was best for me. To see my determination in getting the visa showed that, even though we were different, I was figuring things out my own way. He'd raised a son he could be proud of.

After I got my visa, I had about two months left in Nigeria. I spent that time like I'd spent the previous three years: training every day, practicing with the state team, and collecting checks from the power company.

The day I left for America, I was emotional. I'd fly from Enugu to Lagos, then from Lagos to London, and then from London to America. My father, my sisters, and I got in Stanislaus' car and headed for the Enugu airport. But before that we stopped to see my uncle, Peter, my father's oldest brother, whom we called Chinedu. Because he was the oldest of that generation, seeing him before we left was a gesture of respect. Chinedu hugged me tight, and I realized how meaningful it was for my whole extended family that I was going to America. Chinedu was known around town for always carrying a flute with him and he gave me that flute as a parting gift. Then he said a prayer for me, telling me, "God is with you." That prayer stays with me to this day.

Then we headed off to the airport, where I said my emotional good-byes to my immediate family. I didn't know at the time, but paying for the plane ticket to take me to America had been a source of stress for my dad, who didn't have the money to pay for it. Over the previous few months, from the moment I got that letter from Coach Franson, to the I-20, and even before that—when I was just *hoping* that Egbunike would help get me to America—my dad had always been a voice of caution, pumping the brakes on my optimism. He didn't want to see his son get his hopes up and put all his eggs in one basket—only to see his dreams crushed. Life had taught him a lot of painful lessons. But after I did what I did to get my visa and passport, his attitude changed. He worried about paying for my plane ticket, but he kept that worry from me because he wanted me to embrace my excitement as much as possible. It turned out he'd borrowed money from one of his brothers-in-law, a man named Amobi, and promised he'd pay him back. Three years later I came back to Nigeria for the first time since I'd left. Using money I'd saved from my campus jobs, I paid Amobi back.

All of that was in front of me when I said good-bye to my family at the Enugu airport. I had no idea I would go three years without seeing them. I had no idea what the future held—only that I was excited for it. After my flight to Lagos and then my flight to London, I had a short layover at Heathrow Airport. While looking out the glass window at the gate, I saw the 747 that would take me to Los Angeles. The plane seemed impossibly huge like a skyscraper that had been laid horizontally, and I was astonished that something like that could even get airborne. When the plane took off, I was amazed, just as I was amazed by everything on that flight like the TV monitors showing our flight path, all the different languages being spoken, and the accents people had. The flight was more than 10 hours long, but I didn't sleep a wink.

4

Coming to America

The first person I saw at the airport after I went through customs was Innocent Egbunike. He had a big smile on his face and gave me a huge hug. One year prior at an airport in Lagos, Nigeria, he'd promised me he'd get me to America. He was a man of his word.

Amazed by everything I'd seen, I'd been wide-eyed for the previous 10-plus hours, beginning with the 747 that had taken me to America. My amazement continued after I landed at Los Angeles International Airport. Everything blew my mind. The airport was about 20 times the size of the airport in Lagos, and I couldn't get over how clean it was. It was lined with shops and restaurants; it seemed like a beautiful shopping mall.

Egbunike had picked me up with a friend of his from the track team, Cresencio Gonzalez. He was a middle-distance runner who'd later become one of my close friends. Gonzalez had an old Toyota Corolla from the 1960s, and it was in that old car that we used to hit the American road for the first time in my life for the long drive from LAX to Azusa Pacific. The school was located 40 miles to the north and east of the airport. With four lanes on each side, the web of highways was fascinating to me; it seemed like the pinnacle of an advanced society. I'd never seen that many cars on the road at once. And except for the car we were driving, almost every car was nicer than anything you'd see in Nigeria.

The roads were completely smooth, unlike in Nigeria, where there were tons of potholes. That meant that in America you could drive at the same speed the whole time without constantly slowing down for a pothole. And people signaled when they changed lanes, something you'd never see in Nigeria. And, of course, there was nobody driving out into the middle of the highway perpendicular like I'd seen in Nigeria moments before I was sent into my brother's windshield.

Immediately after leaving LAX, we came down Century Boulevard, and I saw a series of big hotels. I looked at them with amazement. In Enugu, Nigeria, we had a small handful of tall buildings, but seeing so many of them in succession on one road seemed to sum up everything about America: things that were rare and special in Nigeria were in abundance in the United States. Then we passed through downtown, and I saw the skyline, which had actual modern skyscrapers. I admired the beauty and the awesomeness of them. I looked at them and thought I'd gotten off a plane and landed in the future. I'd fantasized about going to America, but seeing the country for the first time had exceeded my expectations. None of it seemed fully real. I felt like I was living in a movie.

I felt the Southern California air right after I got out of Gonzalez's car. It was mid-August, so the weather was warm, but the air still had a crispness. It was nothing at all like in Nigeria, where the weather is like Florida all year round, and the air is humid and full of bugs. In Southern California there were no bugs. Then I looked around and saw the San Gabriel Mountains. Beautiful, majestic. I fell in love with the place then and there. In fact, I have settled there, making it my home for the past four decades.

I slept in a bed that night. And then I did so again every night after that, which was a revelation. I was used to sleeping on mats woven from palm leaves. A bed was a luxury; sleeping in one every night was yet another thing that seemed too good to be true.

Over the following weeks, I walked around the campus and noticed how well-kept the buildings were. Everything in the buildings *worked.* I'm sure 99 percent of the students took this for granted, but I didn't. Soon, I got a job doing building maintenance on campus. I learned that if something breaks it's fixed right away without exception. This was a novel concept to me. In Nigeria, when you give a contract to someone to do a job, it's pretty common for them to just pocket the money and walk away.

When classes started I was confident I'd be prepared academically and I was—my education in Nigeria had been first class. I wasn't the most motivated student or the best one, but I went to class, took notes, and didn't have any problems.

Overall, I acclimated well during those first few months. Being in the nurturing environment of a small college was a good way to make the transition, and practically everyone on campus was nice and helpful to me. That has for the most part been my experience with Americans ever since. Americans are nice, even though I may not agree with everything this country does politically. But it goes back to what I said before about those Nigerian national track camps, where guys from different tribes with age-old rivalries were mixed together: people on an individual level are decent and kind. That's true of Igbos, Hausas, Yorubas, and Americans.

Things settled into a groove pretty quickly. My social circle was mostly the guys on the track team. In addition to Egbunike, there were other international guys on the team, including Blackman Ihem, another guy from Enugu, and we became close. Gonzalez, who was born in Mexico and also played on the soccer team, was a part of our crew. Gonzalez's parents had moved to Southern

California, and on weekends we'd go there and eat the Mexican food they cooked for us. For his part Gonzalez learned some Igbo and hasn't forgotten it, speaking it with us when we all get together. (Sadly, Ihem died of COVID-19 in 2021.)

For the next few years, the track guys became my surrogate family. We were inseparable, especially the international guys. Over the summers, when the American students would go home, we stayed at school and worked campus jobs and trained. None of us had any extra money to be doing much off campus, so our days were spent working six hours at our jobs, training at the track, and hanging out, and we all couldn't have been happier. As for girls? That would come later, when they started to notice me, but that took a while. My first couple of years, I was just trying to get the hang of things and not screw up my opportunity.

At the time Coach Franson was building a powerhouse at Azusa by aggressively recruiting overseas guys and he took us in and looked after us like we were family. On holidays Coach and his wife, Nancy, would have us over for meals. On my birthday I was sitting around watching TV when the Fransons showed up with a birthday cake and a present for me: a collage featuring photos of us Nigerian track guys with him and his family. That was Coach Franson in a nutshell. He was a great person and a great coach, a guy who reminded me of my father. Both were understated, but you knew they were extremely knowledgeable.

Coach Franson's results at Azusa spoke for themselves. We finished second in the NAIA my first year in 1982 and then won the NAIA national titles in 1983 and 1984. In those years big schools like Stanford would host us in dual meets—where one school competes against another—and we knew we'd only been invited because they'd thought we'd be easy competition. But we'd beat those Division I teams, and then they wouldn't invite us back.

*   *   *

The great thing about America—the thing that you don't really see in other countries—is that it's a melting pot. Even with all the racism and xenophobia that's getting stirred up in America today, intolerance is the exception and not the rule. In most cases if you're here, you're friendly, and you work hard, people accept you no questions asked. You become an American. During my first few years at Azusa, I could feel myself becoming one.

A big rite of passage was getting my first car. It was my second or third year. I saved up forever and finally bought an old Honda Accord for $300 from a student from Asia. God knows what year the make was, but the only thing wrong with it was a battery. I stayed at college for five years, and the Honda lasted me the rest of that time, though I was too scared to drive it on the freeway. Still, just by having that car, I was living an American fantasy and I loved it despite its many drawbacks—like the fact that it had no driver's side front window, which meant that I'd get wet whenever it rained. The upside of owning such a piece of junk is that nobody wanted to steal it.

My family didn't own a car when I was growing up, so I had no idea how to be a car owner, and it showed. I didn't know I needed insurance. Had I known I had to pay for insurance, I wouldn't have been able to afford it. Also, I never bothered to figure out the parking regulations, so I'd just park everywhere, getting ticket after ticket. I'd stuff them in the glove compartment and not worry about them. I have no idea what happened to those tickets.

When I graduated after I'd signed my first contract with the Kansas City Chiefs, I gave that car to my friend Ade Olukoju, a younger Nigerian guy on the track team who was behind me at school. It felt like I was passing the torch. It was his turn to become an American then.

Another adjustment for me was the food. If every other aspect of my acclimation was totally smooth, food was the exact opposite. Everything tasted very strange, and it made my stomach churn. The first American food I could tolerate was cheeseburgers. Egbunike got me into them—he vouched for them, I guess—and for several months during my first year they were practically all I ate. I'd go to Del Taco, the fast-food place, and have a bacon cheeseburger at least once a day, usually twice.

There was a Chinese place near campus called something like Chicken and Ribs, and our group of international guys would go there all the time. The spices didn't exactly resemble Nigerian spices, but it was more recognizable than American food. Everyone in America seemed to love the Italian food, but it seemed disgusting to me. (I've since changed my stance.) We became friendly with the people who worked at Chicken and Ribs, and they'd give us bigger portions because they knew we were young athletes in training who didn't have a lot of money. It turned out to be a sound business strategy because whatever money we did have was mostly spent there.

But I missed the food from back home. It took us a while to figure out, but eventually we started cooking our own Nigerian food. The grocery stores in Southern California in the '80s had Mexican and Asian spices, which enabled us to approximate Nigerian spices closely enough. We'd buy frozen okra for our okra soup. Fufu, the starch that's used to scoop up the stew, is usually made from yam in Nigeria, but we used farina and boiled water, then stirred it to form a dough. It wasn't exactly like back home, but it was close enough.

Our food allowed us to share our culture. When we'd go to Coach Franson's house for holidays, we'd cook Nigerian food. And among my teammates, there was a running joke that fufu was my secret source of strength, just like Popeye and his spinach. When I'd have a good throw with the discus, hammer, or shot put, I'd go back to my teammates, nodding triumphantly and say to them, "See what fufu does!"

But for as much as I was enjoying myself, there were times I'd get extremely homesick. I'd realize how far I was from home. Sometimes being in America didn't feel exciting—it felt scary and isolating. I'd get lonely.

I'd think about my mom. In those moments, where I had all the time in the world to cycle through my thoughts and feelings, the fact that she was gone sank in like it never had before. I'd get overcome with grief, which was a strange feeling for me, someone who always considered himself upbeat by nature. Later in life I'd experience clinical depression, and those moments crying for my mom in my dorm room were my first realization of how powerful those emotions can be. In those times I'd also think about my dad, struggling back in Nigeria.

Telecommunications back then were much worse than today; nowadays, I'm constantly on the phone with my brother Chikwelu back in Nigeria. But back then I'd call my dad's office, trying him multiple times because the line would always cut out. When I'd finally get through, the connection was so bad that it would be staticky, then cut out, and I'd have to call back repeatedly. It was nice to hear his voice, but having to struggle so much just to talk for a few seconds made me realize how far away I was from my family.

Mostly, my dad and I sent letters to each other. He'd keep me posted on how everyone was doing, and I told him about America. I would explain how different everything was, how organized things were, how nice the people were to me, and how many opportunities there were. Whenever I'd write those letters, I'd want badly for my dad and my family members to come to America to be able to have these opportunities. They needed to see this. They needed to experience this with me.

Above all, being in America motivated me. Every time I'd see anything new—a skyscraper, a shopping mall, a luxury car—I'd get excited about where I was and think, *I'm a part of this now.* With that excitement came responsibility. My dad had borrowed money to send me here. I was going to seize the opportunity to make him proud.

I got to Azusa Pacific in August of 1982. The Summer Olympics were two years and 30 miles away as the Los Angeles Memorial Coliseum. Back in Nigeria I'd trained with the national team for international competitions, but the prestige of making the Olympic team was on a whole different level. In the world of track and field, the Olympics are the ultimate goal, the dream you have when you first put on track shoes. Getting to Azusa, a stone's throw from where the games were taking place, made that goal seem within reach. I could smell it. That motivated me even more.

I buried myself in the weight room. The fact that it existed right there on campus was a revelation to me. In Nigeria I'd lifted weights, but there was no gym at my high school, and I had to take a bus or catch a ride to the local weight room, which meant I only lifted about twice a week. Now I could lift as frequently as I wanted and I did. Coach Franson wrote weight programs for all of us, but I'd do more than what he wrote. When I got to Azusa, I weighed about 215 pounds. Within months I was at 250.

I loved everything about lifting. I loved being with my friends and cracking jokes. I loved the challenge of getting better, how you could measure your progress, and how your hard work was always rewarded. Soon, I was squatting close to 800 pounds, which is close to what Olympic weightlifters were doing back then. I've always had a drive to challenge myself and I think being in America made that drive even stronger. I'd seen my parents work so hard to provide for us, but they didn't have the resources to do anything but tread water and put food on the table. Now, thanks largely to everything they'd done for me, I had everything I could want at my disposal and had the opportunity to excel. I wasn't gonna let the opportunity go to waste.

And I didn't. The success I had at Azusa Pacific was beyond my wildest dreams. There was not only team success, but also personal success. In the discus, hammer, and shot put, I won eight NAIA national championships as an individual and was a member of four national championship teams. I became the African record-holder in the discus and ranked among the top five discus throwers in the United States. I became the NAIA record holder in the 35-pound weight throw. That throw, as fate would have it, took place at an indoor event in a place I'd never been to before but would become very dear to me: Kansas City, Missouri.

The success made me hungry for more success. It was that positive feedback loop, where seeing the results of my work motivated me to do even more. But for as proud as I was, NAIA titles weren't my primary goal. No, the thing that I wanted more than I'd wanted anything else was to represent Nigeria in the Olympics.

5

OLYMPIC HEARTBREAK

In the United States, track and field gets lost in the shuffle, but in Europe it's a big deal. In Europe there's money in track, which is how I came to be approached by European promoters who'd seen my marks and invited me to competitions overseas. They flew you places, put you up in nice hotels, and paid about 10,000 pounds—more money than I'd ever thought I'd see playing sports.

In 1984 I went to competitions in England and Sweden. Aside from that several-hour layover in London on my flight to America for my first year of college, those trips were my first time in Europe. When I got there, I learned that most of the other track guys had agents and had gotten a lot more money than I did. I wished I'd known better; I just took what the promoters offered me. But really I was just happy to be there.

Some observations about Europe in 1984: coming from America, where I'd been training as much as I could and eating as much as I could, the portions at European restaurants were tiny. In restaurant after restaurant, I'd look at my plate and then think to myself, *That's it?*

Also, they didn't like Americans over there. You could see it on their faces when a group of Americans would walk into a restaurant. They'd be on the defensive immediately, anticipating something rude the American would do. You'd see the same exchanges over and over: Americans would do something to upset the locals—say, making too much noise—the staff would ask them to quiet down, and there would be a conflict. Then, an American would say something like, "But it's my right to be myself." Then the conflict would revolve around the phrase of "my right."

As someone who came to America from Nigeria, I knew what the Europeans were talking about. Americans tend to think rights are absolute things that apply in 100 percent of situations. They don't realize that rights have limits, that nothing is 100 percent all the time, that sometimes people's rights collide, and that we're part of a society where we have to think about balancing everyone's rights. (The response to COVID-19 has brought out this ugly side of American culture.)

But the point of this story, as it relates to my mindset in 1984, was that I had exploded onto the track and field scene and was a budding star. Those trips to Europe signified that I'd reached a level of accomplishment on an international stage. It meant that I was on my way to achieving my goal, which had become my longtime obsession: making the Nigerian Olympic team.

Americans also don't understand that the Olympics are the biggest sporting event in the world. It's bigger than the Super Bowl. In Nigeria and elsewhere in the world, everyone watches the Olympics. If you didn't have a TV, which most people didn't, you found someone who did and crowded into his house. There is no greater accomplishment than being an Olympic athlete or winning a medal. I became an NFL Pro Bowler and the AFC Offensive Player of the Year and I still feel this way.

The '84 Olympics started in late July. It's not bragging to say that by 1984 I had the best marks a Nigerian discus thrower has ever had. Coach Franson had sent my marks to the Nigerian sports ministry, thinking it was a foregone conclusion I'd make the Olympic team. By that point, Coach Franson had become very popular with the Nigerian sports people for having brought over so many guys to Azusa Pacific and he'd go on to become an honorary coach on the Nigerian Olympic Team. But the school year came and went, and I didn't hear anything about making the team.

Other guys, though, heard back. Innocent Egbunike made the team, though that was expected because he was on the 1980 team and was our biggest star in track. But so did some of the guys I'd trained with at the national camp. But I heard nothing. The spring turned to summer, and the weeks passed, drawing closer to the Opening Ceremony. I got antsy. I checked my mailbox every day. I prayed to God that someone would contact me. Coach Franson wrote letters on my behalf, and Egbunike reached out to people back home about me. Both tried to get some answers about what was going on, but nobody had any answers.

In retrospect the most heartbreaking thing is that I maintained my hope until the very end. Even past the very end, as a matter of fact. When I watched the Opening Ceremony from my dorm room and saw Egbunike and the other guys walking into the Los Angeles Memorial Coliseum behind the green-and-white Nigerian flag, I was still convinced somehow that somebody would call me, knock on my door, or somehow I'd join my friends and countrymen on the field when the actual competition started.

Only when I saw the discus competition taking place did I admit to myself it was over. I was in my dorm room at the time. Egbunike was my roommate, but he was at the Olympic Village, so I watched alone. There was nobody around me to cut the sadness. The realization that my dream had died was overpowering. I put my face in my hands and started crying.

Subsequently, I was despondent and adrift. For years the goal of making the Olympics had organized my entire life. And for years every break seemed to go my way. Discovering track and field in the first place and finding out I was good at it. Meeting coach Patrick Anukwa and watching him convince my dad that track would be a good thing for me. Connecting with Egbunike on the Enugu state team, who helped bring me to Azusa. One after another every domino had fallen for me to get me right on the doorstep—literally 30 miles away—of achieving my goal.

What bothers me most now is nobody said anything to me. They could've just written me a letter saying, "Better luck next time." But, no, I heard crickets. It was unprofessional and it's consistent with how the people who run Nigerian sports are lacking. It's a huge country, but it always underperforms in the Olympics. You see guys with Nigerian surnames winning medals for Western countries but not for Nigeria. Compare Nigeria to a country like Jamaica, which is 1/83rd its size yet consistently produces some of the best athletes in the world. Jamaica, a nation of three million people, has won 87 Olympic medals. Nigeria, a nation of 224 million people, has won 27. That's unacceptable.

I really think I could have won a medal. The best mark I ever got throwing the discus was 212', 4". But in practice in the weeks before the Olympics I had thrown one 219. In a big event like the Olympics, you never know how the atmosphere is going to impact you. The adrenaline either gives you an extra boost or throws off your form. But I'd always been at my best in competitions. I'll always wonder what could have happened had I felt that surge of adrenaline on the world's biggest stage. Instead, during the Olympics I was in a daze, staggering around like a boxer who's just taken a punch. Egbunike was at the Olympic Village, where they didn't have anything resembling

Nigerian food, so I'd cook him okra soup with our farina fufu and bring it to him, passing it to him through a wire fence on the outside looking in.

Because Coach Franson was an honorary coach, I went to the Coliseum to watch the games and to cheer on my friends like Egbunike and the guys I'd trained with back in Nigeria. I watched Egbunike win the bronze medal by anchoring the 4x400 meter relay team, which was the first track and field medal Nigeria had ever won. I was proud of him and proud of my other friends who were competing, but being in the stands was painful. It was so close, but it was out of reach. It felt like I was watching my own dream, but I wasn't in it.

*   *   *

So why didn't I make the team? I'll never know for sure. One explanation is that Nigeria had never sent throwers—discus, shot put, or the hammer—to the Olympics, and despite the marks I was putting up, the country simply didn't break with custom. Coach Franson told me that when he spoke to Nigerian officials about me, they'd always say: "We've never had a great thrower before."

"Well, you do now," Coach Franson would respond.

He thought I was a shoo-in. He was as surprised as I was that I wasn't invited.

Another possible explanation—one often floated by others—is that I was Igbo, and the people in charge of Nigeria's athletic programs were not. I've never confirmed this, so I prefer not to dwell on it. But it's no secret that being an Igbo in Nigeria means you didn't get a fair shot, that you're constantly fighting an uphill battle. The ending of the civil war was only 14 years prior to the 1984 Olympics, and the pogroms that killed tens of thousands of Igbo civilians were only 18 years prior. As a 22 year old, that seemed like a long time to me, but maybe the memories of the officials making the decisions were longer.

Whatever the reason was that I didn't make the team, I was crushed. Discus was my life. When I first got into track, I'd actually liked the shot put better, but Coach Anukwa had told me my future was in discus because it involved foot quickness and coordination. Getting the most force possible in just two steps isn't easy or instinctive. It's a delicate dance that has to be perfect. First, your power leg, then your anchor leg, must be timed and positioned perfectly for your trunk to rotate through with maximum force. From your toes to your fingertips, everything has to be in sync. You need quick feet, quick hands, and the ability to be in tune with your body, and Coach Anukwa saw those qualities in me. I rewarded his faith by mastering the sport, becoming better at it than I'd been at anything I'd ever tried. Sometimes, I felt as though this ancient sport, which was one of the sports at the original Olympic games in 776 B.C., had been invented just for me.

But now it all felt like a cruel trap.

When it comes to disappointment in sports, failing to make the Olympics is in a class by itself. In baseball there's always a game the next day. In football there's a game the next week. Even if you lose the World Series or the Super Bowl, there's always next year. But in the Olympics, you have to wait another four years, and, realistically, since I didn't make it at 22, I wasn't going to make it at 24.

A lot of people consoled me. Some people, I could tell, stayed away from me, not knowing what to say. Suddenly, I felt like a failure and I noticed how people tend to stay away from failure. Everything about being me felt different.

I told myself that I was done with track and field. From the sport to the training itself, everything about the discus reminded me of my disappointment and my failure. It was too much; I felt I needed to walk away. Ultimately, that didn't happen, and several months later, when I saw my friends training for the winter season, I joined them. But in August 1984, I had resolved that I was done with track.

But that left open the question: what would I do with myself?

I love sports. That has always been my identity ever since I played soccer nonstop as a kid and my father had to drag me from the field to do my schoolwork and chores. Even at 22 years old, I was still the kid in perpetual motion, a kid who needed to do something.

It so happened there were a couple of guys on the track team who also played football, who always would tell me I should play. "You're strong, you're fast," they'd say. "You'd be great at this."

But it was the last thing I wanted to do. For one thing, I'd see the bruises they'd come back with every day after practice. I'd see them break their arms and tear up their knees. This was supposed to be fun? No, not for me.

Then there was the game itself. I'd been to one football game before and I don't think I'd ever been more bored. Innocent Egbunike had taken me my first year at Azusa. He said, "Let's go to the football game," and I figured he was talking about soccer. When the game started, I saw a bunch of huge guys in pads who would always get together in circles. It looked like they'd whisper things to each other, line up, smash into each other, and then the whistle would blow. Then, they'd do it again.

But after I didn't make the Olympics, I needed a sport to play. It was early August, and football training camp for our small NAIA school was only a couple of weeks away. One morning I knocked on the door of the Azusa coach, Jim Milhon. Coach Milhon knew who I was from track. So he said, "How ya doing, Christian?"

I told him I was interested in coming out for the team.

He just said, "Oh, okay."

Later on, he'd tell me how enthusiastic he was when I first walked in, but he was trying to play it cool, not wanting to turn me off. Then he asked me what position I wanted to play. I didn't know the rules of football, much less the positions. But the night before I walked into Coach Milhon's office, I'd been watching the news, and they played a highlight of Marcus Allen's 74-yard touchdown run from the previous Super Bowl. You know the run: it's beautiful. Allen took the handoff and swept to his left, but there were defenders in his path, so he reversed his field, looped round, and then knifed through the defense untouched on his way to the end zone. It's a play that sticks in your head, a play on which Allen—who later became my good friend—made it look easy.

So when Coach Milhon asked me what position I wanted to play, my mind flashed to that play. I thought to myself, *I could do that.* I told him I wanted to do what that guy had done.

"That's Marcus Allen," Coach Milhon told me. "He plays running back."

At the time I didn't know that running back was a gladiator position where every carry would be like getting into a car crash. I thought I'd just run around and avoid people, and they wouldn't touch me. Another thing I didn't know: with that one conversation, my life had just been set on its course.

6

A New Game

The football program at Azusa Pacific University doesn't exist anymore. It was discontinued after the team didn't field a team during the COVID-19 pandemic in 2020. When I was there, the program ran on a $26,000 budget. Our games usually drew about 2,000 people. Those attendees were some people from the local community but mostly friends and parents of the players. The coach was Jim Milhon, who didn't fit the part of a yelling and screaming coach. No, Coach Milhon was a cerebral guy, a professor of physical education who'd ride his 10-speed bike around campus and bike across the country every summer—from California to New York—with his wife trailing in the van behind him.

In other words, Azusa Pacific was the furthest thing possible from big-time college football, where massive crowds fill the stadium every Saturday, and the coach is a multi-millionaire who's the highest-paid public employee in the state. This meant Azusa was the perfect place for me to learn football because, Lord knows, I had a lot to learn. The first time Coach Milhon handed me a football, I looked at it with curiosity. It was oblong. It was weird. *This* was the ball for the sport Americans were so obsessed with? "Very interesting but very impractical," I said.

I didn't know how you were supposed to hold it or what you were supposed to do with it. The sport was called "football," right? Then how come nobody ever kicked the ball? It's impossible to explain how difficult it is to start playing a sport for the first time at the college level—even at the NAIA, small-college level. Everything that was second nature to my teammates and would be second nature to most Americans who grow up watching football was completely foreign to me.

For one thing, I couldn't catch. Playing catch out in the yard with your dad was not something we did in Nigeria. Everything about handling the ball—catching and carrying—felt unnatural to me. Also, the rules seemed impossibly complex. I didn't know what a first down was. I didn't know how the score was tabulated. It didn't make sense that the defense could tackle someone, but if the offense did the same thing, it was a 10-yard penalty. I didn't know what pass interference was. Sometimes, a guy would come out and actually kick the ball—*foot*ball, right?—but I had no idea why that would happen. Learning the rules would take me years. Even during my pro career, I didn't know them as well as the casual American fan does.

Learning the plays was another daunting challenge. The terminology— odd numbers mean this side; even numbers mean that side—was over my head, a language I didn't understand. The structured nature of the sport itself was alien to me. I grew up playing soccer, which is freewheeling. You pass to your friends, run where there's space, and improvise. In football if all 11 guys don't go exactly where they're supposed to go, the play doesn't work. And I never knew where I was supposed to go.

My friend Joe Schulter was a running back who'd transferred from the University of Utah. He made a cardboard cutout of an arrow, and whenever I'd go the wrong way in practice, which was often, Schulter would lay the arrow down, showing me the right direction. Another time Coach Milhon asked me to block a linebacker if he blitzed. I didn't know what a blitz was, and on the play, the linebacker dropped into coverage. I ran after him, flattening him 20 yards downfield. He looked at me like I was crazy.

A couple weeks prior, I'd been one of the best athletes in the world in the discus and convinced I was going to the Olympics to win a gold medal. Now, here I was a complete novice, always multiple steps behind. It was jarring and very humbling.

When it came time to put on the pads, I had no idea what to do; my teammates had to help me my first few times. When I put on my helmet with all those pads on, I wondered how I was expected to run. When we went out and started practicing, the other guys were running around freely and easily. I felt like I was suffocating. The worst part of it all is when we started hitting each other. I'm not a violent person by nature; I didn't like hitting people and I didn't like getting hit. After our first practice in pads, I was so sore the next day I could barely walk to class. The other guys told me, "It'll get better. The more you move around and get hit, the better it'll get."

But it never did. Every day when I'd wake up, I'd take stock of my body. Everything hurt, and no limb could move without a lot of thought and effort. Every day, I'd think to myself, *They call this sports? Sports are supposed to be fun.* Here's how constant and intense the pain was: I broke my collarbone during training camp but didn't realize I'd done so until weeks later. My broken bone was one of many things that hurt; it just blended into the rest of the pain I was feeling all the time. I only learned it was broken when I separated my *other* shoulder during the season and got an X-ray. The doctor was shocked. "The bad shoulder is better than the good shoulder," he told me.

Then there were the concussions. We didn't know anything about brain injuries, so I wasn't nearly as concerned as I should have been, but I'd bang heads with someone and see stars more times than I could possibly count. This happened every day, multiple times a day. It's not *a part* of the game; it *was* the game. We led with our heads all the time; it wasn't even a question that our helmets were to be used as weapons. When we were blocking, we were told to put our head between the other guy's numbers. My ears would ring for a while, and then I'd get headaches afterward. I talked to one of my teammates about it, and he said the same thing happened to him all the time. It was just another part of this crazy game.

I wanted to quit. I talked to Coach Franson after the first week of practice, telling him I didn't think football was for me. He told me to give it two more weeks. I did and then went back to him after that, telling him I still hated it. He told me to stick it out. "I've been asking about you," he said. "Everyone says you're doing great. You're learning fast. You can't just quit."

So, I stuck it out, even though I didn't like it. I think a part of me was attracted to the challenge. I've been challenged my whole life. Fetching water every day was a challenge. Leaving my childhood home and walking with all of our belongings to go live at an agricultural compound was a challenge. Being an Igbo and seeing your parents denied opportunities was a challenge. Becoming the best discus thrower in Nigeria was a challenge. I take pride in how emotionally resilient I am. When I started playing football, a big part of me wanted to leave because I hated it so much. But another part of me needed to keep trying to see if I could succeed. I needed to know: how good could I be?

Despite my early struggles, there were early signs I had potential. We had a decathlete on our football team named Dave Johnson, who would become famous about seven years later when he was featured in Reebok's famous "Dan vs. Dave" marketing campaign during the runup to the 1992 Olympics. Johnson was a great guy and a phenomenal athlete who had played safety on the football team and, though I don't remember it, he told me a story about how he came to quit football to focus on decathlon. It was during preseason practice, and I got the ball, and Johnson came up from his safety position to meet me in the hole. He channeled everything he had into that collision—and so did I, sending him about six feet back. After that he decided he'd had enough of football. He dedicated himself to track and won the U.S. championship in the decathlon the following year. The rest is history.

My first organized football game was at Occidental College, about 30 minutes west of us. I played three, maybe four plays the entire game, but mostly I watched in a daze. Everything was a blur. The game moved so much faster than it did in practice with so much more violence than in practice. *These guys are actually killing each other*, I thought to myself. Everything was so tense the entire game. After every play someone was yelling. Everything was urgent. I had no clue what was going on. I looked at the scoreboard every now and then and saw some numbers. I didn't know how those points were scored.

Before the game and then again at halftime, I saw guys psyching themselves up in the craziest ways. They'd scream, they'd punch walls, they'd ram their helmets into walls or each other. Meanwhile, I was thinking about my assignments and how not to screw up. I wondered why the other guys were giving themselves a headache before the game even started and before the other team started hitting them. I'd never seen anything like it in sports. Again, where I came from, sports were supposed to be fun.

We lost that first game 21–18, but I didn't remember the result until I was told about it decades later. What I remember is the way I felt. That was my introduction to football, America's peculiar religion. Before I started playing, I had no idea what kind of hold it had on people in this country. Americans need the adrenaline the sport provides. Every March with the previous season a few weeks in the past and upcoming season months away, you can tell people are going through withdrawal. You see the looks on their faces. They miss football. When you talk about football with someone, the look on their face changes, and you know you're getting at something that's very deep for them. The game is a part of the American psyche that's always there but is often suppressed from the surface. Fast. Aggressive. Brutal.

Even with our small crowds, people at Azusa paid more attention to the football team than any other team. But our crowds didn't compare to the crowds you'd see on weekends across the country. When I saw the masses of people in those huge stadiums, it blew my mind. In Nigeria you see those types of crowds when the national team played, but that was only on rare occasions. I'd been in America for two years and I'd learned a lot. But I didn't know anything about my adopted country until I was introduced to football.

With all the technical aspects of the game, all the things I didn't know, I tried to simplify things as best I could. The X's and O's, strategy, blocking, and pass catching could wait. One thing that seemed basic enough was running the ball. I was strong and fast, and the job was to run away from the other guys and not let them tackle me. If I focused on that aspect of the job, I felt I could handle it. I had a size and speed advantage. That was the case my whole career, but in college it was ridiculous. I ran a 4.33 40-yard dash (an unofficial time taken by the Azusa coaches) and weighed 255 pounds. That was faster than the defensive backs and bigger than every linebacker and most defensive linemen. But no matter how big and strong you are, nobody likes getting hit, and the aggressiveness of opponents, who'd played football their whole lives, gave them an advantage; these guys were coming to take my head off. Another advantage was that they knew what they were doing, and I didn't, which gave them an edge for that split-second that determines who gets the best of a collision.

For my first few games, the toss sweep was the play I was most comfortable with. I could outrun anyone, so I'd take the toss and just beat the defenders to the outside. The defenders were always surprised by how fast I was. They were unable to calibrate that a guy my size could be so fast, and every game I'd break two or three long runs. Each of those long runs gave me a little more confidence. I might not have known what I was doing, but speed is the great equalizer, and I had that. (After my first touchdown, I had no idea what to do. So I just stood there in the endzone with the ball. There was no spike or flailing my arms. Finally, it occurred to me I should give the ball to the referee, so I just handed it to him.)

The inside runs I liked a lot less, but our coaches couldn't keep calling the same play to me over and over, so I had to learn how to run between the tackles. I had to overcome my aversion to getting hurt, so I began doing what I did my whole career: talking myself into what I had to do before the play started. *There was going to be contact*, I told myself, and I'd rather deliver the blow than receive it. If I kept my feet under me and ran tough, I'd get the better of the collisions and advance the ball up field. I didn't relish the contact, so I tried to see it in terms of helping my team. Advancing the ball up the field was my goal, and every step was a yard, which meant that every step forward helped my team. Even if I was getting gang tackled, if I kept my legs moving, I was helping my team and doing my job.

With all that in mind, I lowered my shoulder and ran as tough as I had to. I dished out plenty of punishment, and plenty of those NAIA defenders bounced off me, just like they would in the pros. But I never celebrated and never gloated; I wasn't into the macho element of hurting another man or overpowering him. I kept my focus on my technique and advancing the ball forward to help my team.

I was having success my first year, but I wasn't having fun. I thought about quitting constantly and I talked about it with a lot of people. I think it must have gotten back to Coach Milhon because I could tell he was try-ing not to push me that first year. Even when I'd have a long run, he'd sub in for me immediately, not wanting to ride me too hard. If he was strictly interested in winning in the short term, he probably would've kept me in the game. But he was playing the long game. That was a wise move. If he wore me down, I might have quit.

Still, after my first year, I was conflicted about whether I'd play a second year. By that point I was doing track and I was doing very well. I picked up where I left off, and the accomplishments kept piling up. Over the next two years, we won our third and fourth straight NAIA Outdoor Track & Field National Championship, and as an individual, I was the top discus thrower those four years. In 1985 I set an NAIA record with a heave of 208', 4" and in 1986 I was named the Most Outstanding Performer of the NAIA outdoor championship meet after winning both the discus and shot put. With the suc-cess I was having, I let it creep into my mind that the 1988 Olympics weren't so far away. Track may have broken my heart, but I was still in love with it.

So after my first season of football, I told Coach Franson, my track coach, that I wouldn't come out for football the next season. I had tried it just like he'd told me, but now I was certain I didn't like it. I wanted to focus 100 percent on track. But once again, he told me to stay with it. He told me he'd been watching me and had seen how much I'd improved. He said he'd seen some of my long runs, he'd heard people saying I had talent they hadn't seen before, and said that I had a future in football if I stuck with it.

So I did. I wasn't enjoying myself, but I was still motivated to do bet-ter. I was conflicted, but my competitive drive won out. My personality and demeanor are low key, but don't let that confuse you: if I'm going to do some-thing, I'm going to do it to the best of my ability. With that in mind, I studied running backs, getting my hands on tape of some of the best to ever play the sport—like Jim Brown. People had said I ran like him because we were both faster and stronger than the defenders we were going against. Like me, Brown wasn't a rah-rah guy or a yeller or screamer. He ran the ball so much he'd get exhausted, so when he'd get tackled, he'd slowly get up and walk back to the huddle, conserving his energy for the next play. The lesson for me? You don't need to do all of that hooting and hollering and all that macho stuff to be great.

I studied Eric Dickerson and Marcus Allen, two guys who became close friends of mine. Back then the perception was that running backs had to be short in stature, but Dickerson, who was 6'3", and Allen, who was 6'2", showed me you could excel at the position if you were tall. Dickerson wore every pad that had been invented, but Allen wore as few as he could get away with. That taught me there was no one right way to play the position.

I studied Walter Payton, who was so affable and outgoing, yet ran with such ferocity. They called him "Sweetness," and he showed me you didn't have to be a mean guy to succeed or to be a fierce runner. I studied Jim Taylor, the old Green Bay Packers fullback, a punishing runner who always made the defenders pay for trying to tackle him. There was a lesson there: if the price was high enough, the defenders aren't going want to pay it all game, especially in the fourth quarter. I studied the running styles and mannerisms of those great players. Every guy had their own unique style. I was determined to find my style.

I'd get the opportunity the following season. By then Schulter had graduated, so I was the full-time starter. Coach Milhon took the training wheels off, and I had a breakout year, rushing for a then-school record

1,355 yards in just nine games and making the NAIA All-America first team while leading my team to a 7–1–1 record.

My teammates helped; I'll always be grateful for the many guys who went out of their way for me. I've always been a guy who loves the camaraderie of being on a team. And while my feelings on the sport itself were conflicted, I was fulfilled from being a teammate. In particular, Schulter, the Division-I transfer, went out of his way to be helpful when he could have perceived me as a threat. Our fullback, Gregory Johnson, was one of those guys who's a natural talker and teacher and he also took me under his wing. Our team at Azusa was like a large family. I learned a lot from my teammates just like I'd always learned a lot from my older siblings.

Granted, I still wasn't close to understanding the sport—that wouldn't come until long after my playing days—and I still felt at a disadvantage. My size and speed were overcoming a lot of shortcomings, and there were many. I ran too upright, which meant I wasn't running as powerfully as I could have. My stride was too long, which meant I couldn't cut as well as I needed to. My ball handling—switching the ball from one hand to another to protect it when contact came—was sloppy and needed a lot of work, and as a result, I was more fumble-prone than I should have been.

But the more I played, the better I got. Of the 50 plays we'd run in a game during my second year, they'd give me the ball on about 40 of them. I began to love certain aspects of the sport. I loved my teammates, of course, but also the feeling of breaking a long run. You'd hear the crowd and get a rush of adrenaline, like you could feel the people in the stands getting up from their seat. Breaking away from people was exhilarating. There was also this: during my second year, people started telling me that if I kept working hard and kept improving, I could make it to the NFL.

7

Scouts Descend
on Azusa Pacific

Despite my success those first two years, I still didn't think of myself as a football player. It was something I'd fallen into after I'd sworn off track, a rebound relationship after the heartbreak of failing to make the Olympics. But the more distance from 1984 I got, the more I realized that track was still my one true love. After the end of my second year of playing football—in fall 1985—the Summer Olympics in Seoul, South Korea, in 1988 seemed close enough to start thinking seriously about.

By the spring of 1986, I had one more year of eligibility left for sports, but I'd accumulated enough credits to graduate with a degree in physical education. At that point I'd come up with a plan, one that didn't involve football. I'd get my bachelor's degree and become a P.E. teacher at a local high school and in my downtime would train for the Olympics. Of course, I wanted to make the team, but if that didn't work out, I'd settle down to a career as a teacher, which sounded like a pretty good lot in life. Frankly, it still does: a decent salary, good benefits, a pension, and no constant pain or headaches.

But there were so many people, including Coach Milhon, Coach Franson, all my teammates from football and track, telling me to reconsider and stay with football for another year. It seemed like everyone was saying the same thing. "You got so much better from Year One to Year Two," they'd tell me. "If you keep improving, you're a lock for the NFL."

But I brushed them off. Playing professional football simply wasn't something I'd ever pictured myself doing, and even though people were telling me it was a real possibility, I just couldn't come around to seeing it that way. That said, the competitive part of me was intrigued. I gravitate toward challenges—and this was a challenge. And then there was a conversation I'd had with my father about football.

The first two years I'd played, I hadn't even told him. I knew how he felt about sports and injuries, having injured himself playing soccer, a far less violent sport than football. Plus, he'd read articles about American football and he'd tell me how crazy he thought it was that people messed up their knees and got paralyzed playing this so-called "sport." I didn't tell him about playing football because I was afraid of his reaction. He was a man of firm principles and he believed a father's first job was to protect his children—even if they grew up to be 6'3" and 255 pounds.

Still, I knew I couldn't keep this from him forever. So, after my second year and before I'd even talked to him, I just sent him a bunch of articles about myself that chronicled the success I was having on the field. Then I braced myself for what his reaction would be the next time we spoke on the phone. As it turned out, he was extremely proud of me. "You're doing great," he beamed.

I could hear the enthusiasm in his voice. It was similar to how he reacted when I told him about my crazy journey to get my visa. As a father he could be stern and he had a strong sense of the way things should be done. But he was quick to show love and he was always proud when I found my own way in the world. "Keep up the good work," he told me.

That conversation pushed me to keep going in football. When August 1986 rolled around, I showed up to practice determined to see how far I could go. Academically, I added a focus on athletic training onto my physical education degree, but I only took 12 credits the entire year, which cleared my schedule so I could focus on sports.

From the moment I got to summer practice that year, I felt like a man among boys. My instincts for the sport had finally come around. My knowledge of my assignments had become second nature. I no longer had that little moment of hesitation on each play, so I was more assertive and ran with more quickness and power, beating the opponent to the punch. One big skill I'd developed was reading the linebacker on the play side. If he overpursued, I'd cut back on him. If he didn't pursue enough, I'd turn on the jets and beat him to the outside.

For years I'd been working on my running technique and by my third year I'd shortened my stride significantly, which allowed me to run underneath my pads. I'd also worked on my ballhandling and wasn't worried about fumbling. Finally, I felt like a football player and not a track guy who'd been issued pads and a helmet. My stats told the story: I led the NAIA with 1,680 yards and 21 touchdowns, earning All-American honors and leading all of college football with 186.7 yards per game. If I'd done that during a 16-game NFL season, that would've been 2,987 yards. In a 17-game season, that would've been 3,174 yards. It was a great capstone on a college career that would earn me induction into the NAIA Hall of Fame for my achievements in both football and track.

Suddenly, our Azusa Pacific team was a phenomenon. The stands were full, and people were coming early to get a seat in our tiny, 2,000-capacity stadium, and the overflow would be standing room only. Among the many who came to our games? NFL scouts, a lot of them, week after week, to watch me play.

We missed the playoffs, which was disappointing, but it was extremely rewarding to see my hard work pay off with the season I had. I remember one game in particular against San Francisco State University on a rainy day with a muddy field. I ran the ball 34 times that game, and we had the lead, so I kept running and running, grinding down the defense, and running down the clock. I remember thinking after each of those runs: *Give me the ball; I'll do the same thing over and over.* And that's what I did, and it was an amazing feeling if you're wired to be a competitor like I am. You're doing exactly what you want to do, and nobody can stop you, even though they're trying as hard as they can. It's the best feeling you can have in athletics, and the great thing about football is that it's a shared feeling. The offensive line was hyped up, and I have a vivid memory of the camaraderie in the huddle with the rain coming down. We couldn't wait for the next play to start so we could keep our success going.

In retrospect that game was a preview of the feeling I'd get a few years later in 1989 when Marty Schottenheimer came to the Kansas City Chiefs. And the foundation for my pro success was laid in that final year at Azusa.

*   *   *

Because I wasn't taking many classes, I had time to train harder than ever before. I practically lived in the weight room, doing squats, cleans, inclined presses, bench presses, leg curls, leg extensions, lat pulls. I became a machine, cleaning 315 and squatting 725. I was also running constantly. I did all kinds of sprints, including the 40-yard dash because I was trying to improve my 40-time for the scouts. I'd do shuttle runs like crazy: five yards and touch the line, then 10 yards and touch the line, then 20, then 30.

I've always had an ability to be self-motivated and to push myself past limits. I'd think about it like this: if you don't want to do something, you think about how tired you're getting. But if you're doing something you want to do, your focus becomes not quitting. You want to finish what you've started because you decided you wanted to do it in the first place. My parents had always taught me that if I ever did things halfway, those habits would follow me for the rest of my life. I watched my parents do everything they had to do to provide for us, and their lesson stuck with me. I had a chance to become a pro football player and I wasn't going to do this halfway.

People were noticing. The scouts came from all of these American cities I'd only heard about. It was like a different fantasy future life every day, and I found myself constantly daydreaming about what my life would look like in a few months. The Kansas City Chiefs visited four times, the most of any team. The Buffalo Bills and Washington Redskins visited three times. The Cincinnati Bengals, Indianapolis Colts, Pittsburgh Steelers, Miami Dolphins, Tampa Bay Buccaneers, New York Jets, and San Francisco 49ers also visited.

I had in my mind that my first choice was the 49ers and wanted them to draft me. I didn't really follow pro football, but I knew the 49ers were a premier team, and there was a comfort factor in that they played in California. I'd seen parts of their games on TV and had noticed they ran a split-back offense, which was similar to the one we ran at Azusa, so my thought at the time was that the offense suited me better. (I was wrong about that; I somehow missed that they threw to their backs more than any other team, and catching the ball was the weakest part of my game.)

The 49ers were one of three teams to fly me in for a pre-draft visit; the Los Angeles Raiders and Houston Oilers were the other two. I remember meeting Bill Walsh, and it was like meeting a professor of football. His demeanor was studious, and everything in his office—the chairs, the furniture—was white. I knew Walsh's reputation and I saw a whiteboard in his office with plays sketched on them. They were the most intricate plays I'd ever seen. Then he and I talked for about an hour. He asked me questions about how I came to America, whether I enjoyed football, and how my track background helped me as a player. It was some version of the question everyone was asking me: *Was I actually serious about football?*

After I spoke with Coach Walsh, the 49ers brought in Dr. Harry Edwards, the famous sociologist who worked as a consultant for the team. His questions got deeper into my background—about my parents' personalities, the dynamics between my siblings—and I sensed that he was trying to get at what made me tick. I was impressed by how advanced everything with the 49ers was. To them, football was serious business.

The Raiders' visit was a lot more informal, showing that there's more than one way to have success. Al Davis met me and showed me around the facility, and we chatted the whole time. He wore his trademark white track suit and sunglasses, and his hair was slicked back, which didn't move unless the wind blew. After we watched practice together, he had just one question for me. "You've seen these guys practice and you've seen their size and speed," he said. "Do you think you can play with them?"

I told him, of course, I could play with them. "I have size and speed, too," I said.

Then I went to Houston, where the Oilers had arranged with the Houston Rockets for Hakeem Olajuwon, my countryman, to meet me at the airport and host me. Olajuwon was a couple of years younger than I, but he was already a superstar. I'd first heard of him in college, when he was the biggest name in college basketball, leading his University of Houston team to back-to-back appearances in the national championship game. I was at Azusa Pacific by then and I'd watch those NCAA Tournament games just to watch Olajuwon. He was one of us and was making us proud.

He met me at the Houston airport and couldn't have been nicer. We cruised around Houston in his Mercedes and then we came to the house he was building in Sugar Land, which was on some sort of body of water, and we stayed in the guest house while the main house was under construction. It was an eye-opening moment for me about the money in American professional sports. Olajuwon was a Yoruba, a guy with humble beginnings from Lagos, Nigeria. He'd come a long way.

The best part of that visit was seeing how everyone around town loved him. Every restaurant we went into or on the street, wherever he went, people lit up when they saw him. "What's up, Dream?" they'd say, and he was friendly to everyone. Olajuwon's a personable guy, but he's low key a lot like myself, and I thought it was cool how everyone loved him but also gave him his space and let him be. That was a good model for how to be an athlete; I wanted to emulate that.

We stayed in touch during that visit and remain friends. Not long ago, I was playing golf in a celebrity charity tournament hosted by Marcus Allen when I was approached by Clyde Drexler, the Hall of Famer who'd played with Olajuwon at the University of Houston and then reunited with him later in his NBA career to win a championship with the Rockets. "Next time you talk to Dream, tell him that I always used to kick his ass in Ping-Pong," Drexler told me. "He'll deny it, watch. But it's true."

I spoke to Olajuwon after that and passed on Drexler's message. "He's lying!" Olajuwon said, just as Drexler predicted. "He never beat me!"

In Houston I got a tour of the facility and met coach Jerry Glanville. He was funny and charismatic, the type of guy who's entertaining every time he opens his mouth. We talked for a bit, and at a certain point, he looked me in the eye and asked abruptly, "Hey, Christian, can you play in the NFL?"

I laughed because I'd heard this before. "Yeah, I can play in the NFL," I told him.

*   *   *

Back at school my calendar was getting so packed that I wasn't working out alone anymore; all of my workouts became showcases for the scouts. Every day for weeks, someone would show up with a stopwatch and try to time me. It was getting ridiculous. So at a certain point, Coach Milhon designated Wednesday as the day I'd work out for scouts, leaving me the rest of the week to train by myself. The scouts came with their stopwatches and their poker faces. It was clear they were there to gather information, not tell me how great I was. They all said some version of the same thing: "Keep working. Keep learning. We'll see what happens."

It was clear there were many doubts about how my abilities would translate to a level of competition where I wasn't bigger and faster than everyone. I needed something to put those doubts to rest. That's what our sports information director, Gary Pine, was working on, tirelessly. His mission was to get me into a postseason showcase game. He called all of them—the

Senior Bowl, the Blue-Gray Game, the East-West Shrine Bowl—and kept calling and calling. None of them were interested.

Then, I caught a break. Paul Palmer, the star running back at Temple University who'd played under young head coach Bruce Arians, dropped out of the game, opening up a spot. A few days before the game, Pine called me and asked if I was ready to fly to Mobile, Alabama, on short notice and play a football game despite not having played for more than two months. I told him I was ready. Because of my track background, I was never not training, so I was always ready. I flew to Mobile. It was one of those things that seemed like fate—like the dominos that fell that day when I got my visa. God seemed to be paving the way for me, as if I was being told that if I kept working hard, God would take care of the rest.

But when I got on the practice field in Mobile, I did a double take when I saw the size of the players. The linemen were all 300 pounds. I'd never seen such a display of huge guys in my life. Everyone there was big, and everyone there was an athlete. We only had a week to practice, but the playbook contained more plays than we had in our whole playbook at Azusa Pacific. It was obvious this was a different level than the one I'd just dominated.

During the first practice that week, a guy on my team sprained his ankle and he got sent home, and it was obvious how disappointed he was. We all knew that you didn't want to be the guy who got hurt and got sent home. That would cost you hundreds of thousands of dollars as your draft position plummeted. As it happened, I sprained my ankle the next day and I was worried sick. More than anyone else there, I needed to prove myself against this level of competition. All that week, I got treatment on my ankle, but it wasn't responding well, and I was worried. While in the trainer's room getting taped, I said to the trainer: "When do you think they'll send me home?"

His answer surprised me. "Nobody's sending you home," he said before explaining that there'd been newspaper stories about me: the big Nigerian guy who was shockingly fast and who'd set all kinds of records at an NAIA school. I was now the Senior Bowl's big attraction, he told me, and that there was no way they'd send me home.

That put my mind at ease. My ankle improved, and I enjoyed the rest of the week, making friends with some guys who'd go on to become great NFL players like Cornelius Bennett from the University of Alabama and Alonzo Highsmith and Vinny Testaverde from the University of Miami.

Don Shula was the coach of our team. I'd heard his name, but it wasn't until I got to practice that week that I realized what his name meant to people—the Super Bowls, the perfect 17–0 season in 1972, the wins he was piling up on the way to becoming the NFL's all-time leader. When that man talked, the whole room went silent, and everybody listened. He didn't raise his voice once to us all week because he didn't have to. I didn't have to be an NFL historian to understand that this man was a legend who commanded respect.

That week was also my first exposure to the crush of the media. I'd dealt with the occasional reporter at Azusa, but I never saw so many at once. At the Senior Bowl, they were a pack—and they all had the same questions over and over: "How did I learn about football?" "How did I get so big and fast?" "Was I scared to go against these big guys after facing lesser competition at Azusa?" I answered their questions patiently and politely. The experience would serve me well because I'd deal with the media a lot more starting very soon.

Then the game started. It was jarring going against guys who were so much bigger and faster than what I was used to, so I had to remind myself that *I* was a bigger and faster back than what *they* were used to. I told myself this was yet another challenge that I'd have to embrace; I talked myself into staying in the moment.

I scored four touchdowns, a Senior Bowl record that still stands. The first three were from one yard out, and the last one was a six-yard run where I trucked a linebacker into the endzone and put the game away for our team. The final score was 42–38, which remains the highest combined score for a game in Senior Bowl history. After that game I was on the map. There were many doubts about me going in, but that game began to answer a lot of them. The accolades and write-ups came pouring in. I was the Offensive Player of the Game, and it seemed like I was all anybody was talking about. Years later, I'd get inducted into the Senior Bowl Hall of Fame.

This was the end of my college career, and after the game, I called Coach Milhon and Coach Franson, the two guys who'd encouraged me to stick it out during the tough times when I wondered what I was doing playing this crazy game. For years they were in my corner, constantly delivering the same message: "Just stay the course and do your best. Everything will work out the way it's supposed to."

They'd been right all along. I was on the verge of becoming an NFL football player.

Scouts had told Coach Milhon I was likely to go in the first or second round, but I tried not to get ahead of myself and I mostly tuned the speculation out. By this point I was firmly in the mode of rolling with the punches. Whatever happened, I'd make the best of the situation.

On draft night a bunch of teammates and I gathered at Coach Milhon's house. His wife, Dot, who was like a den mother to all of us, made her famous lasagna, which was the dish she'd always make for the football players. There were a couple of local TV stations at the house, and they trained their cameras on me the whole time. It felt a little weird, but I was taking it all in and eventually I got used to the cameras and settled into the festive mood of the night.

Sometime late in the first round, the phone rang, and Coach Milhon answered and handed it to me. It was someone from the Kansas City Chiefs, though I don't remember the guy's name. He said, "We're thinking of drafting you, but we wanna make sure you wanna play football. Are you sure you wanna play football?"

I told the guy yes. It was a version of the same question I'd been asked a hundred times since the whole draft process started. My answer was always the same. "Okay, hang tight," the Chiefs staffer said.

About a half hour later, the guy called again. They were going to draft me, but they wanted to make sure one last time: "Is this what you want?"

It was. With that, I became a Kansas City Chief.

We all started celebrating at Coach Milhon's house, high-fiving and hugging. Coach Milhon told me that, wherever my career and life might take me, he'd always be there for me—and he has been. At the time he said he'd wanted me to go to the Chiefs because he thought they had the best uniforms in the NFL.

I was just happy to be drafted by someone. And it was Kansas City, a city to which I'd actually been and had athletic success. Kansas City hosted the annual NAIA indoor track and field championships every winter, and in February just weeks before I was drafted, I set a then-NAIA record by heaving the 35-pound weight 66', 5".

Kansas City also had a place in my mind for another reason. Several years before that at the indoor championships, I was surprised to learn that the 35-pound weight throw was actually outside that year. I was dressed in my shorts and, when I came out for the throw in the dead of winter, I was so cold I thought I was going to die. Ultimately, I ran back into our team van and changed into a pair of pants someone had loaned to me, but I'd never been cold before and I was traumatized. I decided that the cold wasn't for me and I feel the same way to this day.

But I'd have to make peace with the cold because Kansas City was where my journey had taken me. After the draft the Chiefs flew me to the team headquarters, where I was swarmed by reporters. The Chiefs, I later learned, had traded up 11 spots to draft me, and when I looked at the papers the next day, there was a lot of skepticism about that move. Everyone seemed to call me a "project." I took some offense to this. *Hadn't I just set the NAIA record at Azusa the year before? Hadn't I proven myself in the Senior Bowl?*

I resolved to prove everyone wrong. I was eager to start working on becoming the best NFL player I could be. The Chiefs drafted me early in the second round after drafting Palmer, whose injury had allowed me to participate in the Senior Bowl, with their first-round pick at No. 19. It was clear they wanted talent at the running back position after finishing either last or second to last in the league in rushing every year from 1983 to 1986.

Soon after the draft, we got our playbooks for minicamp. It was a smaller playbook than the one we'd get for the regular season—maybe 20 pages compared to the textbook thick thing they gave us for the season—but I buried myself in it, making a point to get all my assignments down cold by the time minicamp started. I remember how I'd felt stepping onto the field for the first time in college and I remembered the cardboard arrow that Joe Schulter had placed on the ground because I didn't know where to go and what to do. I wasn't about to let the same thing happen in the pros.

8

CHIEFS LEGENDS

My first offseason with the Kansas City Chiefs gave me a lesson in the organization's deep, rich history. The franchise had won in the past and expected to win again. Our owner, Lamar Hunt, was proud of that history. So after I got drafted, he made a point of introducing some of the team's all-time greats to some of the draft picks. It was my honor to meet them.

The late, great Len Dawson was my friend. He was always cool, always friendly, and always supportive of me. At the beginning of my career when there was so much skepticism about me, Dawson went out of his way to show that he believed in me. He was our color commentator on radio broadcasts and hosted HBO's *Inside the NFL*, and it seemed like he always picked the Chiefs to win and always mentioned that I was the reason he was picking them. He'd been retired for a long time, but it felt like he was still the Chiefs' quarterback and would always be. Dawson is in the Pro Football Hall of Fame and—like all great quarterbacks—he had a way of pumping up his guys with confidence.

His death in 2022 made me very sad. We had become pretty close over the years because we both spent time around the Chiefs organization when I came back for games and charity events. Apparently, Dawson had been suffering from dementia after a 19-year career in the pros, but I thought back on the last time I saw him, when we'd sat in a suite together during the

2018 season's AFC Championship Game, and he didn't seem compromised to me. This was the game we'd lost to the New England Patriots. On a crucial play late in the fourth quarter, Dee Ford's offside penalty negated an interception that would have sealed the game for us, and afterward everyone was on Ford's case. But Dawson wouldn't have it. He kept saying Ford was an excellent player who was one of the reasons we were among the league's elite teams in the first place and then he listed a bunch of mistakes the Chiefs had made that day. That was the essence of Len Dawson: he was a born quarterback, a born leader, who knew that football is the ultimate team game where everyone's in it together.

I also met Dawson's favorite passing target, Otis Taylor, a premier receiver of that era who should be in the Hall of Fame. If Taylor played in today's game, he'd catch 120 balls a year. In 1987 he was working for the Chiefs as a scout. He was extremely knowledgeable and was always in the locker room giving us tips about opposing players. Sadly, Taylor is one of the guys who has felt the full impacts of the sport. For decades he has suffered from Parkinson's disease and dementia and in recent years he'd been bedridden before passing away in March of 2023.

Through no fault of his own, Taylor was involved in an infamous incident in 1987, my rookie year, during the players' strike. Linebacker Jack Del Rio, who played for the Chiefs at the time, was picketing outside of Arrowhead Stadium and when Del Rio saw Taylor walking into the stadium, he mistook him for a replacement player and began shouting at him, which eventually escalated to a physical attack. Taylor wound up suing Del Rio, and the two later settled out of court. I always got along with Del Rio, but years later when he made his comment referring to the January 6 U.S. Capitol insurrection as a "dustup"—as if trying to overthrow an election and trying to murder political opponents is the same as two opposing football players shoving each other after a play—I thought back on that incident with Taylor. I know Del Rio has long wanted the USC head coaching job, but given those incidents, it's not surprising to me that USC has steered clear.

Another Chiefs legend I met before my rookie year was Hank Stram. By 1987 the former Super Bowl-winning head coach was 64 years old, but he was still the same character he always was on those NFL Films clips. He was chatty, quick-witted, funny, and all the players enjoyed having him around.

Another guy with a big personality was Ed Podolak, who was on the 1969 Super Bowl-winning Chiefs team and became the franchise's leading rusher until I broke his record. (My record has since been broken as well.) Podolak was fun-loving, someone who was always cracking jokes. He was loud, had a big smile, and didn't seem to give a crap about any consequences. As a runner he was just as fearless, which is probably what made him such a good player. When I was breaking his all-time rushing yards record, Podolak was really cool about it and supportive of me. His whole thing was that running backs have to stick together. "Records are meant to be broken," he told me. "Shit, I broke someone else's record!"

Willie Lanier was just as good of a guy but had the opposite personality. Lanier's quiet, serious, and doesn't mince words. He'll tell it to you straight—whether you like it or not. During his Hall of Fame career, he became the NFL's first Black middle linebacker at a time when many people thought Black people weren't smart enough to handle such an intellectually demanding position. Lanier destroyed that racist myth, and his status as a pioneer might explain the chip on his shoulder. There's no doubt about Lanier's intelligence. For many years he has been a very successful financial advisor in his native Virginia.

Buck Buchanan was another Hall of Famer on that defense in the '60s and '70s and another guy I was introduced to after being drafted. Buchanan was a gentle giant; he was 6'7", and it seemed like he'd just glide into the locker room, like he was a football god among us. Sadly, Buchanan got lung cancer during my career and died in 1992 at just 51 years old. But his wife stayed in touch with the team and became a member of the Chiefs Ambassadors, our alumni group. She has a firecracker personality that balanced out Buchanan's cool demeanor. Now she's one of us and she keeps Buchanan's spirit alive.

Buchanan and Lanier anchored that Chiefs defense along with Bobby Bell, a Hall of Fame linebacker and defensive end who's an even better person. Among former Chiefs players, Bell has become famous for a magic trick he does. He'll ask if you if you have a quarter, and if you do, he'll have you put it in your palm. Then, he'll place his hand under yours and say "Go!" When you open your palm, your quarter's gone. For decades Bell has taken everyone's quarters from them. We used to joke that you always knew when Bell was coming because you'd hear the quarters jangling in his pockets. Bell and I became close and remain so. He's a warm guy who always lets you know he's there for you. He does a lot of charity work and in 2022 he was the annual honoree for my charity, the Christian Okoye Foundation, which helps underprivileged kids. Bell's an emotional person, who doesn't hide how much he cares about other people, and when he got on stage to accept the award, he broke down in tears.

Speaking of community work, the late Walter White had some great years for the Chiefs in the '70s and then became one of the organization's most active alumni. He is the only one of the legends I discuss in this chapter who's not in the Chiefs Hall of Honor, but he should be. White was the guy who started the Chiefs Ambassadors, an organization for former players to do charity and community outreach. I'm very involved in the group and come back to Kansas City a few times a year to do events, including speaking at schools and charity fund-raisers. The causes are important, and it's important for me to stay connected to the city where I made my name. Without those fans my career doesn't mean much.

As a player I got involved with charity work early on and made a point to spend most of my Tuesdays—the typical day off for NFL players—going into the inner city to speak with kids at schools. Kansas City, like all places in America, is divided socioeconomically and racially. I remember early in my Chiefs career driving east of Troost Avenue and noticing the roads weren't nearly as well-maintained; it was obvious that when you crossed Troost, you were on the Black side of town. Growing up in a poor family in Nigeria, I know how hopeless things can sometimes seem when you're poor, so I made a point of going to schools to connect with kids. To have a famous person telling them that there's more to life than their daily struggles, that they can accomplish great things, can flip a switch that changes their lives is hopefully inspiring. Goal setting and working toward something often doesn't seem realistic to them. To meet someone who came from poverty and accomplished his goals can change their entire outlook. I've always considered this kind of work my obligation. That remains true in retirement, and I spend most of my time working with the foundation.

The Chiefs Ambassadors are such an important part of the organization that when the Chiefs won Super Bowl LIV, Chiefs owner Clark Hunt gave rings to us. It means a ton to me and it shows how similar Clark is to his father, Lamar Hunt, in how he consistently does the right thing and respects the people who wore the Chiefs uniform. I met Lamar before my rookie year and liked him immediately. He came up to me, shook my hand, and said, "Welcome to Kansas City. You're going to love it here."

He was absolutely right, and a big part of that was the tone he set for the organization. He was a gentleman, a soft-spoken guy who had no ego whatsoever, which is remarkable considering his accomplishments. He reminded me of my dad in how genuine and wise he was. After I won the Mack Lee Hill Award, which is given annually to the Chiefs' top rookie, I brought my dad over from Nigeria for the first time to attend the team awards ceremony. Lamar spent practically the entire evening with my dad, asking him questions about himself and his life in Nigeria. It was such a respectful gesture. It was the mark of a good man who was interested in people and cared about them.

I don't think people fully appreciate what an influential historical figure Lamar was and what a force for good he was. Something that Chiefs fans should be proud of is that he was a pioneer in the integration of professional football. Long before anyone else was doing it, the Dallas Texans, who then became the Chiefs, signed a lot of Black players. Lamar hired Lloyd Wells, the first Black pro football scout. They were ahead of the curve in drafting players from historically Black schools like Lanier from Morgan State, Buchanan from Grambling, Taylor from Prairie View A&M, Gloster Richardson from Jackson State, and Emmitt Thomas from Bishop College. It's no coincidence that the league's first Black middle linebacker—Lanier—was a Chief. It's no coincidence that in 1969 the Chiefs became the first NFL championship team with a majority of Black starters. Stram also deserves a lot of credit for being way ahead of his time on race relations.

Lamar is credited with coining the term "Super Bowl," which he named after a ball his children used to play with. He also was one of the founders of the AFL and the primary architect of the AFL-NFL merger. In 1984 the trophy given to the winner of the AFC Championship was renamed in his honor. During the Chiefs' recent era of excellence led by Andy Reid and Patrick Mahomes, they've won three Lamar Hunt Trophies as of this writing, which is a great tribute to his legacy. Meeting those Chiefs legends after being drafted showed me there was a history of winning here and that the franchise was counting on me to help get back to winning. I soaked up that history—and I was determined to make some of my own.

9

WELCOME TO THE NFL

My first professional contract gave me a signing bonus worth $250,000 and a first-year base salary of $125,000. By today's standards that's peanuts. But it was more money than I'd ever dreamed of seeing. I'll be honest in a way most athletes aren't: the money was a big reason I played, a big part of my motivation. How could it not be? I spent my childhood eating one meal a day while my country was fighting a civil war, and my uncles were on the battlefields. Deprivation was very real to me, just like it is for many athletes from forgotten places in America. The more money I made, the further removed I was from poverty—and the more opportunity I had to help my large family back in Nigeria.

I played six years in the NFL and never had many extravagances, but during my rookie year in particular, I lived a very simple life. Through a recommendation from our public relations department, I got an apartment in Independence, Missouri, about 15 minutes from the stadium on I-70. It was a two-bedroom place; I slept in one of the bedrooms and in the other bedroom I basically threw a bunch of junk that I didn't know what else to do with. My days mostly consisted of going to practice and coming home. My life was regimented and monotonous because I was just trying not to screw up. Even though I had my signing bonus, I was still fearful the Kansas City Chiefs could cut me at any moment—and I was determined to provide for my family as much as possible and for as long as possible. Besides, I'm not much of a drinker or a partier and, even though I was single at that point, I was still pretty shy around women.

I didn't buy a car, but a local car dealership—I can't recall the model—approached me and Paul Palmer, my fellow rookie running back whom the Chiefs had drafted in the first round that year, and offered us cars free of charge as kind of a sponsorship thing. (Palmer's great guy; nearly three decades after we were together, I still talk to him on the phone a few times a year.) So I wasn't the kind of guy who blew through my signing bonus with fancy cars, expensive clothes, or a huge house. The one indulgent thing I did with my money—the one fantasy that I played out—involved food.

I'd been in the U.S. for five years, and it had been hard to find goat meat, which was my favorite kind of meat back home. But in Kansas City, a guy I befriended told me about a farm and meat market in De Soto, Kansas. I went out to the farm and was told to select a goat, which I did, and then I was told to come back in a couple of days. When I came back, the goat had been slaughtered and processed into bite-sized chunks I could put in my freezer. That single goat powered my rookie season, nourishing me for months. Nearly every day that year, my routine was to come home, cook a meal that reminded me of home, and go to sleep. It was a no-frills lifestyle that allowed me to focus on my job, which I intended to hold on to. And it worked. That rookie season, I rushed for 660 yards, was named to the Pro Football Writers of America's All-Rookie Team, and earned the Chiefs' Mack Lee Hill Award given annually to the team's best rookie.

*　*　*

Whatever success I had that season would have seemed like a pipe dream during my first few days of training camp at William Jewell College in Liberty, Missouri. When I first saw my new teammates on the field, I took one look at their speed and size and trembled. Every single guy was huge. Every single guy was an elite athlete. Throughout the pre-draft process, I'd been asked countless times if I could hang with bigger, faster athletes—and if I really wanted to be an NFL player. I'd answered yes every time and was sick of the questions. But now I wasn't so sure.

In those days training camp was six weeks of two-a-days—far more than the two weeks we did in college—and that kind of workload has been banned in today's NFL for a decade. Camp was miserable. I'd always considered myself an extremely hard worker, but I'd never worked so hard before or been brought to the point of exhaustion and misery so often. The collisions were like nothing I can even describe. It felt like getting into multiple car crashes each day. Every practice there would be injuries. I'd develop friendships with guys, but then they'd get injured or cut and I'd never see them again. This wasn't college, and it certainly wasn't the friendly, Christian, small school I'd attended. By coming to the NFL, I'd entered a new, brutal world.

The heat in the Midwest in late August is unbearable. I knew heat and humidity from Nigeria, but I'd never played football with the helmets and pads in that kind of weather, having only played in the mild climate of Southern California. After every practice I'd lose 20 pounds just from sweating and then I'd have to consciously drink water until I went to sleep to replenish those fluids.

Mentally, camp was just as draining. Back at Azusa Pacific, we'd had just four running plays; we'd run them to either side, and I could run those plays in my sleep. The Kansas City Chiefs' playbook had about 100 plays with all kinds of permutations. The mental jump is an overlooked hardship in going from the small-college level to the NFL. It was even more difficult for someone like me with such a limited background in football. Adding to my stress was that I was convinced the Chiefs just might cut me at any moment. I was naive; I didn't know how uncommon it was for a team to cut a player they'd just drafted in the second round. Even if I had known that, I would have assumed that if anyone drafted so high could ever be cut, it would be me.

Did I think about quitting? Of course I did; it's human nature. At night in bed, when I'd be too exhausted to move, I'd think about leaving camp under cover of darkness while everyone else was asleep. But then I'd think about Coach Milhon and Coach Franson and everyone who'd supported me at school, doing everything they could to help me learn football because they saw potential in me. I thought about my parents, who busted their asses every day for me and my siblings without getting a check like I did for $265,000. I needed to keep going. I owed it to all of those people. And I needed the money. My only option was this: I resolved to do everything with 100 percent effort. After practice I would study my playbook; I was committed to get the entire thing down cold. On the field, I'd sprint every moment of every play and do everything with maximum physicality.

It was exhausting. I'd run the ball seven times and after that I'd hardly be able to breathe or see because there was so much salty sweat coming down from my helmet into my eyes. My eyes stung; everything hurt. I kept having the thought I'd had my first few weeks of college football: *Aren't sports supposed to be fun?* But quitting was not an option. I'd either make it or I'd collapse from exhaustion on the field.

Somehow, I got through it. Not only that, I thrived. Early in training camp, Paul Palmer had been getting the bulk of our carries. Palmer and I were on the field at the same time, but I was mostly blocking for him. But as camp wore on, I started getting those reps. By Week One, when we opened up at home against the San Diego Chargers, I was the primary ballcarrier.

* * *

My first impression of Arrowhead Stadium was that it was beautiful. I loved the design of it; it was so graceful and sleek. I loved the atmosphere before the game. There was a sea of people in the parking lots and tailgates as far as the eye could see. I loved that the seats were red and the fans wore red and the team wore red. It felt like we were all one: the city, the fans, the players.

One thing I didn't love was the artificial turf. It felt like playing on concrete, but AstroTurf was what was fashionable in those days, so I reverted to the mindset I'd used so many other times in life and resolved to make the best of the circumstances. Turf allowed you to cut sharper and get more speed, and with my punishing running style and my speed in the open field, I could use the turf to my advantage.

That's what I did in the second quarter against the San Diego Chargers. We were leading 3–0 and had the ball on the Chargers' 43-yard-line. I took a toss to the right and noticed that the defense had overpursued, which was one of the things I'd mastered in college: diagnosing overpursuit and then cutting back against it. I pushed off the turf, burst through the seam in the defense, and then turned on the jets. As I ran downfield, I felt like I was flying. I didn't hear any of the 57,000 people in the stands that day because I was completely immersed in what I was doing, which was sprinting 43 yards into the end zone. It was the longest run for the Kansas City Chiefs franchise since 1985.

Only when I crossed the goal line did I hear the roar. I was used to playing in front of crowds of 2,000 at Azusa, but that roar from a packed NFL stadium was powerful. I hadn't experienced that kind of passion and support before, and it pumped me up. When I heard the sound, I wanted to hear it again. I rushed for 105 yards that day in a 20–13 win. I was looking forward to hearing that roar plenty more times in the coming weeks.

Unfortunately, that didn't happen.

The following week, we traveled to Seattle and got blown out by the Seahawks. Then, the season stopped abruptly. Strife between labor and management had come to a head, and the players went on strike. We were gone for 24 days. It was an ugly, tense time and a debacle for the players. We had sought free agency and a new collective bargaining agreement (CBA), but the owners wouldn't budge, and we returned to work without an agreement on free agency or even a new CBA. The only thing we had to show for the strike were a lot of missed paychecks.

The whole thing was poorly planned. Because we went on strike at such an early point in the season, the owners were able to field replacement teams to get through the early slate of games. These games were televised by the networks, which had lucrative contracts that went back to the owners so the owners didn't lose much money, but the players did. The smarter approach for us would have been to wait until late in the season in the weeks before the playoffs because that would've hit the owners where it hurts. They would've been much more reluctant to trot out replacement players for late-season or playoff games than the early-season games.

The whole thing was a mess from the beginning, which I blame on poor leadership from the National Football League Players Association. Consequently, the players weren't sufficiently united—15 percent would ultimately cross the picket line—and the owners knew this and exploited it, essentially waiting us out until we came back with our tails between our legs. The strike was such an embarrassment for the players that the union was decertified; it took until 1993 until it was formed again. (By then, a series of court cases had given NFL players free agency.)

Things got really heated between the players. A lot of guys had families to support and mortgages to pay and they were angry about losing a decent-sized chunk of their prime earning years for what they believed was a doomed cause. Back then NFL players didn't make nearly as much as they do now, and many guys were living paycheck to paycheck, hoping to squeeze as much money out of their short careers as possible. To other players the strike would work if and only if there was solidarity among players. They were angry with the guys who questioned the strike, believing that undermined the cause.

Personally, I was conflicted. I supported my union's general position because, even though I didn't know much as a rookie, I knew that NFL players were treated poorly compared to athletes in other sports, and we needed to fight back. But even then I knew the timing was awful. Fortunately, I had recently received my signing bonus and I didn't have major expenses, so I could afford to ride it out. I'd go back and forth between Kansas City, where I'd train with my teammates, and California, where I'd hang out with friends from Azusa. A part of me felt that after the whirlwind of my previous few years, the strike provided a nice mental break.

Back in Kansas City, I joined my fellow union members picketing outside of Arrowhead Stadium when the replacement players came to work, but I didn't approve of how far some teammates took things. Some guys sat in the back of pickup trucks, brandishing rifles. I had sympathy for the replacement players, who I assume needed the money as desperately as many Americans do. As for the guns, I'd seen in my early childhood how quickly things can escalate into unspeakable violence. When you've lived through an actual war and seen dead bodies on the side of the road, you don't enjoy seeing guys in pickup trucks carrying guns.

So I have a lot of mixed feelings about the '87 strike. But one thing I'm not conflicted about is it failed because of poor union leadership—something that remains a problem with the union today. DeMaurice Smith makes about $3 million a year, but retired players are thrown into desperate situations left and right because they don't have health insurance. I've heard too many stories about guys who had to sell their houses or Super Bowl rings to cover procedures from injuries sustained during their careers. I've heard too many stories about guys who've had to file for bankruptcy, hoping to keep it a secret. These tragedies mostly happen out of public view, but when you run in the circles I do, you see this stuff all the time. And the union leadership doesn't seem to have the motivation to change it.

*   *   *

When we finally got back to football after the strike, I did well individually, but our team's season went down the drain quickly. Our replacement players lost the three games they played, and then we came back and dropped our next five, putting our record at 1–9. Our final record was 4–11.

It was the first time in my life I'd ever dealt with losing like that. At Azusa Pacific we were a winning team, and in track and field, I controlled whether I won or lost. In football you're one of just 11 guys on the field at a time, but I tried to focus on controlling the things I could control, which was my own performance. Even while I was having success, I still feared in the back of my mind that it could end at any moment, that the league would figure out I was an imposter, that I'd somehow be exposed. That fear kept me motivated.

Winning the Mack Lee Hill Award gave me an occasion to invite my father to the United States for the first time, so that he could attend the awards ceremony. He and my brother Emmanuel came to the ceremony. Seeing my dad looking happy and fulfilled in his tuxedo and deep in conversation with Lamar Hunt was a very proud moment for me. After I'd gotten my signing bonus, I was able to convince my dad to stop working, even though that was against his nature. My dad had worked so hard for so long to put me in a position to have this opportunity that I wanted him enjoy life. Watching him at that banquet, I could tell that was exactly what he was doing.

My dad and Emmanuel stayed in the U.S. for about a month with me that offseason, mostly in a new place I'd just bought in Claremont, California, where I lived in the offseasons for several years before buying my current place in Rancho Cucamonga. (I settled in that part of Southern California, which I still call home because all of my people from Azusa Pacific were there.) I wanted my dad to stay in the U.S. permanently, but he wanted to spend his retirement years in his home country, so at a certain point, I stopped trying to convince him. Emmanuel, though, wound up staying in California, getting his master's degree in business administration from Azusa. He went on to work in the business department of UPS for more than three decades before retiring last December. With my brother included, I had a network of Nigerian people in California, and with every passing year, that was beginning to feel more like home.

I was also building a network in Kansas City. After I came to the Chiefs, a Nigerian-born banker named Frank Olipo, who lived in the area, contacted me through the Chiefs' public relations office, and we became good friends. Olipo had heard of me and figured I wouldn't know anybody in the area—and he was right—so he introduced me to the small Nigerian community in the area, taking me to parties and dinners and showing me around town. It was Olipo who told me about the farm in De Soto, where I got my goat. Olipo also introduced me to a Nigerian restaurant in Kansas City, and on many Monday nights during my time there, we'd eat dinner together and have our egusi and okra soups, and the flavors and his company gave me a warm feeling of home.

As word about me spread, other Nigerians in NFL cities would reach out to me. When we were in our hotel the night before the game, many times people would drop off Nigerian food for me at the team hotel. In retrospect, I probably shouldn't have eaten food like that from strangers, but I always did and I always enjoyed it.

My teammates, though, introduced me to Kansas City barbecue. Gates was the spot all the Chiefs players frequented. I won't lie: barbecue took some getting used to because I wasn't accustomed to all the sugar. But once I developed a taste for it, I didn't look back, and during my career, Gates became my go-to spot as well. I used to eat a lot of chicken back in Nigeria, so I prefer barbecued chicken—I've never quite understood why Americans are so infatuated with ribs—though I like the burnt ends at Arthur Bryant's.

These days I'm into Jack Stack since there's one near the hotel I stay at when I come into town.

During my early playing days as a pro, another person who really looked out for me was my running backs coach, Billie Matthews. On the field, he was patient with me, knowing I was new to the system and new to the complexity of an NFL offense. Off the field, he'd often have me over to his house for dinner with his wife. And I was very close to my fellow running backs like Paul Palmer, Herman Heard, and Larry Moriarty. All three of those guys couldn't have been nicer. Heard and Moriarty were the veterans, and everyone knew the team had drafted Palmer and me with the plan of getting rid of the older guys, but both took me under their wings and helped me at every opportunity, and I'll always be grateful for their professionalism. Palmer, who became my close friend and was nicknamed Boo-Boo, was a fun-loving guy whom everyone enjoyed being around. I became the main running back, and he was eventually waived, but there was never any feeling of competition between us, which says a lot about what a good person Palmer is.

My teammates and I would go to Kansas City Royals games after practice (in what was then called Royals Stadium) because it was right across the parking lot from Arrowhead. I'm not much into baseball, but it was impossible not to appreciate the deep baseball tradition in Kansas City, which included the founding of the Negro Leagues. Over the years I met Buck O'Neil several times at various events, and it was obvious how beloved he was as the keeper of that history. And while I never found the sport itself so compelling, going to Royals games was fun for two reasons: one, the stadium itself had gorgeous fountains, and the upper deck sloped downward in such a pretty fashion. And two, Bo Jackson.

You really had to be there to understand what a huge deal Bo was in Kansas City; he was a legend pulling off the unheard of feat of being a great player in two professional sports. Bo was an athlete who made other athletes stop and watch, and we used to love watching him play just to see him move on the field. Even when he would strike out, he'd do something amazing like break his bat over his knee or even his head. The town went crazy for Bo, and even though in 1987 the Royals were two years removed from their World Series victory, people still talked about it all the time. It was one of those things that made me realize that if we could ever start winning, the fan support in Kansas City would be unbelievable.

Unfortunately, we didn't win much my first two years in Kansas City. After going 4–11 in my first year, we went 4–11–1 in my second year. After that second season, head coach Frank Gansz was fired. That year got off to a bad start for me when I shattered my thumb in a preseason game at Arrowhead. I was trying to run for a touchdown, but as I went to stretch out the ball at the goal line, a guy game down on my arm, smashing my thumb into the rock-hard AstroTurf. It was a pretty gruesome injury that would require surgery during which doctors put six pins in my thumb to piece it back together so it could heal. It was the first of many surgeries I would undergo because of football injuries.

When I returned to action, I hurt my back. Then, later in the season, I broke my hand. Overall that season I played only nine games. When I did play, I played pretty well, rushing for 473 yards on 105 carries, and my 4.5 yards-per-carry average was actually better than my rookie year figure of 4.2. But it was a disappointing season for both me personally and the team.

By the end of the second year, the losing had started to get to me. The weather would be freezing—I hate cold weather now but hated it even more back then—and I'd be getting pounded into the AstroTurf. I'd daydream about the offseason, when I could go back to California and not have to get my ass kicked every week. Football players are human.

Plus, as the season wound down, the crowds at our games became smaller and smaller, so that Arrowhead seemed cavernous with huge swaths of empty seats. The organization always gave us tickets to distribute to family and friends, and by the end of '88, it became embarrassing how little anyone wanted them. I'd call Olipo and invite him to the game, and he'd try to be polite and say, "Ah, I have plans!" Despite the rich history and the legends who'd played there decades ago and were still involved with the organization, there was no energy around the franchise those last few weeks—and for good reason.

Internally, though, we knew we weren't that far away. Our defense had premier players, especially in our secondary with Albert Lewis, Deron Cherry, and Kevin Ross. We had a promising rookie with obvious talent at defensive end named Neil Smith. Overall, our defense finished 10th best in fewest yards allowed in the NFL. But the offense was vanilla. Teams had no fear of us, and defenses seemed to know exactly what was coming.

Our head coach, Gansz, was a very nice guy who'd been an excellent special teams coach with the Chiefs and who'd later win a Super Bowl in that role with Dick Vermeil's St. Louis Rams. Gansz was so popular with the players that they'd advocated for him to become the head coach after John Mackovic was fired after the '86 season. But as a head coach, Gansz was in over his head. Our team lacked an identity and an edge.

After the '87 season, an investigative piece in *The Kansas City Star* came out revealing that for years Gansz had misled people about his military service, making it seem like he'd been a fighter pilot when in reality he'd never seen combat. We remembered all the stories he told about being a fighter pilot. His nickname even was "Crash," and he'd even brought in John Glenn to speak to the team once. We all liked Gansz and didn't enjoy seeing him embarrassed by that article; we felt sorry for him, not betrayed. Gansz was fired by our new general manager, Carl Peterson, who'd been hired late in the '88 season.

At that point the Chiefs franchise had hit rock bottom. We knew there was talent on the team, but that talent wasn't translating into wins, and the franchise seemed directionless. We needed someone to change that.

10

Martyball

I was back home in California during the offseason in 1989 when I got the phone call. It was my new coach, Marty Schottenheimer. He told me it was nice to meet me over the phone, but he needed to meet me in person. To *see* me. The Chiefs bought me a plane ticket to Kansas City, and I was in Schottenheimer's office before I knew it. The expression on his face when he first saw me said: *Wow.* It's one thing to hear a guy's 6'2", 260 pounds, but it's another to be in the room with him. Our meeting lasted all of two minutes. He told me his plan for the 1989 season was to run the ball and run it a lot. "How do you feel about that?" he said.

I said I was good with it. Even two years in, I was still not totally comfortable with the finer points of the game like blocking and route running. But running? That I could handle. He asked me, "Are you sure?"

I told him I was. And when he asked me how many times I could carry the ball, I said I could handle more than 30 carries a game. "Good," Schottenheimer said. "Prepare yourself to run the ball."

I was back in California that same day, but Schottenheimer's message got through to me. During my first two years, I'd shown promise, but now it was time to make good on it. Now it was time to establish myself in this league—and to get some financial security for myself and for my family back home. At the time I was playing under my rookie contract with a base salary that had increased to $225,000. A part of me was bowled over that someone could make that much money playing sports, but another part of me knew that was chump change compared to what other running backs were making. My goals in football were simple: I wanted to play as long as I could and as well as I could, so I could help my family as much as possible. With the opportunity for a big second contract on the horizon, I had a lot riding on that season. When Schottenheimer told me this was my chance to have a big year, it sharpened my focus during the offseason. I trained harder than ever.

When I first got to the NFL, I noticed that the way I train and the mentality I brought to it made me unique among players. Driven by adrenaline and anger, most guys listen to rock or rap. But I listened to Bob Marley's "Three Little Birds" and classics like that. With my background in track, especially in the discus and shot put, I knew that training was all about getting in tune with your body and being aware of all your subtle movements. I didn't need angry music to pump me up; I just needed to relax and concentrate.

In addition to weight training, I'd spend four hours on the Azusa Pacific field, practicing running with the ball in my arm. People think of running with the football as an instinctive thing, and that's true, but what they don't realize is that it's possible to train your instincts. So with the San Gabriel mountains as my backdrop, I'd put cones down and do change-of-direction drills over and over, training myself to run low and underneath my pads, feeling the subtle shifts in bodyweight when I'd cut. When I ran to the right, I held the ball in my right hand. When I ran to the left, I switched hands. My track background gave me confidence I'd be able to develop the muscle memory to make these techniques second nature when the games started. I listened to my mellow music and went to work.

When minicamp started in May, even though we were a team coming off the second most losses in the NFL during my first two years, you could feel the optimism around the Chiefs. And it revolved around our new head coach. Schottenheimer had taken the Cleveland Browns to the AFC Championship Game in 1986 and 1987 and then went to the playoffs again in '88. But a dispute with ownership led to his exit from Cleveland. The Browns' owner, Art Modell, told him he needed to relinquish playcalling duties, and that didn't sit well with Marty. The Browns' loss was our gain, and we knew it.

Schottenheimer had a vision for the way the game should be played. "Martyball," it was called. He emphasized using a physical, straightforward running game to control the clock, playing good defense, and wearing down the other team so to grind out tough wins. When he came to Kansas City, he wanted me to be the lynchpin of that vision, but first he needed to make sure I could be that guy. When he called me into his office in the offseason, he wanted to confirm my size and physique were as advertised. And on the first day of minicamp, he wanted to see about my speed.

We all ran 40-yard dashes, and the coaches clocked me at a 4.36. Even though I'd been clocked at a 4.33 in college, Schottenheimer was surprised and he double-checked with his assistant coaches to make sure they had the same time. They all did. Then Schottenheimer made me run it again just to confirm everyone's stopwatches weren't deceiving them. I did and clocked the exact same time.

When we got to summer training camp and started practicing, it became obvious I would be the focal point of our offense. The workload would be a lot, but I was always in great shape, so I was happy to take it on. I knew instantly I'd enjoy playing for Schottenheimer. When he'd talk to you, he'd put both hands on your shoulders and look you in the eyes. He was direct and confident and didn't waste words. My first impression of him was to think to myself, *This guy knows exactly what he's talking about.* That impression never changed. He was the best head coach I've ever had.

I also hit it off with our new running backs coach, Bruce Arians. A fun-loving guy who had a great rapport with his players, Arians was in his first season in the NFL after coming from Temple, where he'd coached two of our running backs, Paul Palmer and Todd McNair. (McNair would later serve as Arians' running backs coach with the Tampa Bay Buccaneers when they defeated the Chiefs in Super Bowl LV.) Even though Arians had coached McNair and Palmer previously, he didn't favor them and was very fair and patient with me. We're still friends, and years later he told me that he always respected how self-motivated I was and that he never felt the need to motivate me because he knew I'd do my job.

Everything was in place for a big season for me, but one day in camp, all of that excitement vanished in an instant—and was replaced by terror. We were doing the "bull in the ring" drill, an old-school football drill in which one guy, the "bull," stands in the middle of a circle surrounded by other players. At the coach's silent signal, a guy on the perimeter charges at the bull, and the bull has to locate the onrushing guy and brace for contact before the guy flattens him. It's a violent drill that had the aim of making us tougher—part of the mentality Schottenheimer was instilling in us.

During this particular practice, I was the bull. When I turned around at the last instant to collide with the guy rushing at me, we hit each other at an awkward angle. My entire body collapsed in a heap; I couldn't feel any of my limbs. I still remember the terror of trying to move but not being able to. It's a bizarre, freaky sensation; communication between the mind and body is cut off. I remember the panicked voices of my teammates: "C.O., get up, man!" I remember Arians leaning over me with a concerned look on his face.

It lasted about 15 seconds, maybe 20, but it seemed like an hour. I tried to move but couldn't. I tried again, but I couldn't move. Again and again until I began to lose hope. Finally, I felt a cold sensation that washed over my whole body. Then, I was able to move my legs. Then, feeling returned to my entire body. It was a "stinger"—a common injury that sounds harmless enough but one that in my case was actually nerve damage that would get worse and worse every single time I carried the ball. After the stinger I started taking indomethacin, developing a tolerance that led to years of addiction. I've had three surgeries related to my spine and have experienced severe weakness in my legs the past two decades that make me cling to banisters when I walk down stairs. The constant pain I've lived with for years is frankly more than the average person can comprehend. All of it traced back to that moment. If I knew in 1989 what I know now, I might have walked away from the game right then and there. It's something I think about a lot and feel conflicted about. But at the time, I was told by the doctors that it was a minor thing. I believed them, and my focus was getting back on the field. I missed the rest of training camp and played sparingly in our opening game, a 34–20 loss against the eventual AFC champion Denver Broncos, but by the second game, I was the starting running back and carried the ball 27 times.

In reality, my body was already falling apart. But I *looked* more imposing than ever. After my injury the Chiefs' doctors designed a fiberglass addition to my shoulder pads so my neck wouldn't snap back. I was already one of the biggest backs in the league, and the addition, which most people mistakenly thought was a neckroll, made me look even bigger. I couldn't lift my hands above my head to catch the ball and that year I only had two receptions. But it didn't matter because I could still run the ball and I was about to do a lot of that—just like Schottenheimer had said.

*   *   *

This is no overstatement: the 1989 season turned the Chiefs franchise around. We went 8–7–1 that year after two straight horrible seasons. We didn't make the playoffs, but we came close, giving the fans something to get excited about at long last.

Excitement is what had been lacking at Arrowhead Stadium the previous two years. If you can picture it, Arrowhead, now known as the most raucous NFL stadium, was a ghost town. In our last three games of the '88 season, our attendance was in the 30,000s—and that was the *listed* attendance because at any point in the game it looked like there were about 10,000 people there. That changed in '89 with Marty Schottenheimer as our new head coach and—just as importantly—Carl Peterson as our new general manager, a position he held for 20 years. They made it clear they didn't see a long rebuilding process. They saw our defense, saw our offensive line, saw me, and thought we could win now. The Chiefs soon began a run of leading the league in attendance and of consecutive sellouts, even though Kansas City was the sixth smallest television market in the league. That love affair between city and team, which you see today, was rekindled in '89. With Schottenheimer and Peterson, we finally had an identity: nobody would be tougher than us. Nobody would make the opponent earn it more. Nobody would hit harder.

I can pinpoint the exact moment when things turned around. It was our fifth game of the season. We were 1–3 and we went into Seattle to play the Seahawks, the defending AFC West champions who were known for their physicality under coach Chuck Knox. The Seahawks jumped on us early, bringing back the opening kickoff for a touchdown and then opening up a 16–3 lead.

Early in that game, I suffered another injury. Seattle's Kingdome had some of the worst AstroTurf in the league—really, it's insane that they made us play on that stuff—and I tripped on a fold in the turf and fell awkwardly on my shoulder, and it felt like I was falling onto concrete. On impact my shoulder popped out of its socket, ripping the ligament clear off a bone and jarring loose a small piece of my bone off as well. The injury was severe and would require surgery after the season. It compounded the pain from the nerve damage in my neck.

But I played through it, and in the third quarter, our team was still behind 16–3. We drove to their 13-yard line, and our quarterback, Ron Jaworski, called a running play to me. It was a "check with me" play, which meant Jaworski would tell us the direction of the run at the line of scrimmage. But there was a problem because the Kingdome was famously loud—especially when the opposing offense was near the goal line and the fans were on top of us—and I didn't hear what Jaworski said. I guessed it was going to the right, but I guessed wrong, and the resulting confusion threw off the timing of the play, which meant all the defenders had gotten off their blocks by the time I got the ball.

But that didn't mean that the play was over. Schottenheimer had told me something repeatedly since the beginning of training camp that stuck with me: "If you can't find a hole, make one." He instilled that in me like a mantra. So in Seattle I did as told, bursting through the first tackle attempt and then running over two more guys while charging toward the end zone. Four more guys had a clean shot at me, but I ran through them all, going into the endzone standing up.

The touchdown pulled us within six points; we'd go on to win the game and avoid being knocked out of contention early in the season. On the day I rushed for 156 yards.

This was the template. This was Martyball. This was the mentality Schottenheimer was instilling when he said, "If you can't find a hole, make one."

That was my mindset all year. I led the league in rushing and also set a Chiefs franchise record, running for 1,480 yards. I did it on 370 carries, which also led the league and was also a franchise record. (Larry Johnson now holds both records.) I scored 12 touchdowns, earned All-Pro honors, and was named the UPI's Offensive Player of the Year for the AFC. When Schottenheimer had called me at my home in California early the offseason, he'd essentially told me to be ready to have a big season. I listened to him and I did.

As a team we also internalized that Martyball mindset, priding ourselves on wearing the other team out. We led the league in time of possession, averaging more than six minutes of possession more than our opponents. We played complementary football, knowing we had an outstanding defense, which finished second in the NFL in yards allowed. Our defense was headlined by two young, outstanding pass rushers, Derrick Thomas and Neil Smith, along with our stars in the defensive backfield: Albert Lewis, Kevin Ross, and Deron Cherry. For the first half of the year, we were 3–5, but in the second half, we went 5–2–1. For those last eight games, nobody in the AFC had a better record than us. Those free tickets I once could never give away? They were suddenly in high demand.

With our defense and running game, we were always in games, which meant there was always something to keep fans engaged. And the fans responded. The 1989 Kansas City Chiefs might have missed the playoffs—a tough home loss against the San Diego Chargers in the second-to-last game of the season knocked us out—but we gave the city something to rally around. Chiefs Kingdom woke up and has been awake ever since.

Kansas City is a small town by NFL standards, and it was amazing to feel the passion people have for the Chiefs, who are a civic institution. I noticed this passion immediately. At the time the only other American city I had to compare it to was Los Angeles. On the West Coast, there are too many other diversions—Hollywood, the clubs, the beach—for the city's passion to take hold like it does in K.C. Nowhere is that passion more evident than at Arrowhead Stadium. It's the best atmosphere in professional sports hands down: the acres of tailgates in the parking lot before the game, the sea of red in the stands, the intensity on every play when the game starts. It's unbelievably loud. I *still* don't quite understand how the fans are able to generate so much noise in an open-air stadium. As a player you feel the support, which gives you a surge of positive energy. Because of K.C.'s small-town atmosphere, it's almost like your big, extended family is in the stadium. You want to perform for them.

That family atmosphere carried over after the game. As I got more comfortable in the city, I started engaging with the fans more. On Sundays after the game, I'd come out of the locker room and see—or rather smell—the barbecue the tailgaters were cooking up. I'd stop by and chat with the fans and eat some chicken and drink some beers with them. Where else but in Kansas City does that happen? The people are down to earth and straightforward. Midwestern values. I got along with them because I'm the same way.

I was halfway around the world from my home country in a city I'd never heard of until several years prior. Culturally and weather-wise, it was a long way from Nigeria. And yet with the way the fans embraced me and the team that season, I felt like I was home.

* * *

I was also at home in Marty Schottenheimer's offense. It was based on simplicity. That suited me because even in my third pro year I was still learning the intricacies of the game. Here's what we did: about 80 percent of the time, we'd run the same basic off-tackle play. The only variable would be the side we'd run it to, which was determined by a "check with me" call by the quarterback at the line of scrimmage. Just that small advantage over the defense—we knew where it was going, and they didn't—gave us an edge. In that brief moment of indecision for the defenders, we'd overpower them. We ran that off-tackle play over and over. Schottenheimer would always say: "The defense knows it's coming, even the fans know it's coming, but still nobody can stop us." It was power football at its simplest and best.

Specifically, my job was to read the play-side offensive tackle's head during his block. If the tackle's head was to the outside of the defender he was blocking, I'd run outside of him. If it was to the inside, I'd run inside of him. I lined up 7.5 yards deep in the back-field with no blocking back in front of me like I'd had in our previous offense under Frank Gansz. This allowed me some space to generate downhill momentum. Not having a lead blocker in front of me gave me an extra beat to survey the blocks and determine where I was going.

By that point, I knew exactly what kind of runner I was. My running style was…straightforward, shall I say? I didn't dance; I was too big anyway. If the play called for the run to be off tackle, that's exactly where I was going. If the hole was clogged up, there was going to be a collision, and by then I'd learned that was to my advantage. I had force on my side—the mass times acceleration of a 260-pound guy coming at them with 4.4 speed and a 7.5-yard head start.

The simplicity of our offense allowed us to master the details. Schottenheimer was very detail-oriented, always coaching me on my footwork and body positioning, knowing it's the little things that determine whether a running play is successful or not. When you see a big back like me run someone over, it looks like the runner's natural ability is merely taking over, but the fact is I practiced this stuff constantly. Like our offense, I didn't do a lot, but I mastered the details of what I did.

The same goes for our offensive linemen. Every lineman who has ever played football prefers run blocking to pass blocking because in the running game the offensive lineman is the aggressor, and in the passing game, it's vice versa. The linemen loved our new smashmouth style. As a result, they performed better.

That year it all came together, and before I knew it, I was a phenomenon. My nickname—"The Nigerian Nightmare"—caught on and took on a life of its own. It originated during a film session during either my rookie or second year. There was a clip of me running the ball in the open field one on one with a defensive back who clearly wanted no part of me. I was in that situation countless times and I remember the scared, darting look the opposing safety or cornerback would get in his eyes. He was pissed the defense had broken down so that he had to make the tackle. You could see him calculating how to make a passable attempt at tackling me while absorbing as little contact as possible because no human wants to be in a violent collision with someone who outweighs you by 70 pounds. We watched the clip in the film room. One of our quarterbacks, Bill Kenney, a friend of mine who'd go on to become a Missouri state senator, said, "Man, you're a defensive back's worst nightmare!"

Without missing a beat, Irv Eatman, our right tackle and another friend of mine, chimed in: "The Nigerian Nightmare!"

It had a ring to it; it stuck. In my opinion it's one of the great sports nicknames of all time, and I'm proud of it. At the time, I'm sure many football fans had barely heard of Nigeria, so I was happy to introduce my country to America. It was also a stamp on my career. Many NFL players— battered and forgotten—come and go in anonymity. But I had a nickname people still remember me by.

It was a storybook American success story: guy who nobody had heard of comes from a faraway place and becomes an overnight sensation. People loved the backstory about me not knowing anything about the game until a few years before. Sudden fame is weird. Things just…started happening. All of a sudden, people were recognizing me in restaurants and paying for my meals. The Costacos Brothers, who made these fun, over-the-top themed posters in which star athletes dressed up, flew me out to Seattle and put me in a Freddy Krueger glove holding a shredded football. They were playing off the "Nigerian Nightmare" and *A Nightmare on Elm Street* connection; the poster also featured guys dressed up in the uniforms of our division rivals, cowering in a bed out of fear of me. I also filmed a radio commercial for Campbell Soup's chicken pot pie. Evidently, people loved the way I said the words "chicken pot pie" in my precise Nigerian accent. Even today people still come up to me and tell me they remember the commercial and the way I recited those words.

Being famous was especially strange for me because of where I came from. Kids growing up in America dream of being a celebrity because the dream is constantly dangled in front of them. They're told, *This could be you!* But for me growing up in Nigeria, being famous was totally outside the realm of possibility. That wasn't a dream for a Nigerian boy growing up seeing dead bodies by the side of the road in a war-torn country.

All of the new attention was interesting and nice, I guess, but I kept it at arm's distance. By 1989 I'd moved from my apartment in Independence, Missouri, to a condo in quiet Blue Springs, Missouri. My evening routine during the season was always the same: I had dinner, watched some TV, and went to bed. The only way I knew how to handle fame was to keep being myself. I accepted the blessings, thanked God for them, and kept working hard. I was having a career year, but I'd been around long enough to know life in the NFL can be humbling.

*   *   *

At the end of the season, I was voted to the Pro Bowl. It was my first Pro Bowl; I'd make one more after the 1991 season. They put us up at the Hilton Hawaiian Village in Honolulu, and I flew out Coach Franson and his wife Nancy and put them up as a token of gratitude for all they'd done for me. The week was paradise. We'd have practice in the morning, but it wasn't very long, so we'd be free by about noon, and every night there was a luau on the beach. One of the cool things about the Pro Bowl is that the players meet each other and form friendships. For me it was cool hanging out with some of the guys I'd only heard about and seen on TV like Joe Montana, Jerry Rice, Boomer Esiason, Howie Long, Thurman Thomas, and Eric Dickerson.

Dickerson would go on to become one of my best friends; I see him often in Southern California to this day. He's a what you see is what you get kind of guy, and I've always respected that because I'm the same way. We clicked immediately and now we're like brothers. I tell Dickerson things I wouldn't tell anyone else and vice versa.

We had a lot of downtime in Honolulu. So that week, Dickerson and I were hanging out and decided to go to the beach, but I had to swing by my room to put on my bathing suit first. I went to my room, and it so happened that there'd been a delivery to my room of a huge bag of Zubaz clothing. You remember Zubaz, right? The zebra-striped gear, which was flowy and stretchy with bright colors? In 1989 I guess the company was just trying to get a foothold among football players because I had no idea all that stuff was coming. But I saw the bag and unpacked it and I needed a pair of pants to put over my bathing suit, so I grabbed a pair of Zubaz pants in Chiefs colors and threw them on. I liked them; I thought they looked pretty cool.

Dickerson knocked on my door. Something you need to know about Dickerson was that he was into the way he looked. He was into his look on the football field—his style was iconic—and he was into his look off it. He's a man with style, no question. So when I opened the door and he saw me in the Zubaz pants, he burst out laughing. That describes our friendship. Dickerson is a fun guy to be around and he always gives it to me straight.

More than anything, Dickerson is loyal. He loves his friends and his family and supports them through anything. I know if I'm going through something, he is just a phone call away. He's extremely wise and is a person of great empathy. Since retiring from football, I've often had a hard time with public speaking at the many charity appearances I do. I'll often get up on stage and search for the right words, but I'll feel the gears in my brain screeching as they turn, struggling to come up with something. I don't know what this is about—Nervousness? Brain injuries I sustained playing football?—but it happens to me all the time and it's very uncomfortable. Some of these public appearances are with Dickerson, so he has been in the crowd when I get up to speak. A couple of times when I've looked at him, I could see his body movements, and it was almost as if he was urging me—or willing me—to find the right words and get them out. I've never told him this, but I want him to read it in this book: I've seen him doing that, and it means a lot to me. I feel his desire to support me. I feel his love.

Dickerson and I play a lot of golf together with another former NFL player, Chris Hale, who played for the Buffalo Bills' AFC championship teams. I give him a hard time about losing those Super Bowls, and he comes back at me that I never even *went* to a Super Bowl, which is fair. Hale is a real outgoing guy with a magnetic personality. Everywhere he goes, people love him. I'll even bring him to Kansas City to hang out, and people are always asking me about him after. The last member of our golf foursome is Brad Booth, a retired firefighter and great guy.

Anyhow, all of the success that came my way in 1989 was fun. But along with the success came physical pain. A lot of it. Defenses were now keying on me every game. I got the ball all the time—and because I hardly ever went down after the first hit—it all added up to a lot of collisions. I enjoyed many things about being a pro football player, but I can't say the game itself was ever fun to me. Truth be told, even with the success I had, I never loved the sport. I suspect this is true for many NFL players, but nobody says so publicly.

To me, football was always a job. I wanted to help my family by making money and I also wanted to do a good job for its own sake. I'm a hard worker, a guy who takes pride in getting things right, a guy who takes pride in being reliable, even courageous. But I'm not a violent person and I never found the violence of football fun. American kids are different. They watch football on TV, so they get it ingrained in their minds that the game's violence is thrilling. But I didn't grow up around the game. I saw it differently—in a more clearheaded way, I think.

That season, 1989, was the year that put me on the map. That NFL at 100 commercial they always show, where I become Jim Brown, who becomes Walter Payton, who becomes Red Grange, who becomes Alvin Kamara, who becomes Barry Sanders, etc., well, I'm in that commercial because of '89. But that was also the year that set me up for the lifetime of pain I've endured ever since.

After the injury I suffered in the bull in the ring drill, every time I lowered my shoulder and hit someone, I felt a shock of severe pain. Imagine someone putting a knife in your shoulder muscles and twisting it. The pain would last a few seconds and then fade. By the time the next play was called in the huddle, it was gone. But very often that next play was a run to me. And every time I had a conversation with myself: *This pain will be awful, but you have to do it. You can't tip-toe into holes. There's only one way to do this. Either you do it or you don't.*

People see a guy my size and think I'm indestructible. But just because I was big and just because I inflicted a lot of pain on the other guy doesn't mean I didn't feel pain myself. I pushed through it. The doctors had told me my neck would be protected by my big shoulder pads; I trusted them. What I didn't know was that my nerve was messed up beyond repair and I was risking catastrophic injury with every carry. After I retired and started having problems, doctors took one look at it and told me how lucky I was that I didn't get paralyzed. I'm like a lot of guys who played in the NFL. I was led to believe there was *pain* and there was *injury*, and they were two different things and that what I was feeling with my neck and shoulder was merely pain. But what I was led to believe was wrong.

11

THE GAME THAT
CHANGED EVERYTHING

Looking back, it astonishes me how violent the game was when I played. Watch any game on YouTube and you'll be shocked at how physical it was. It was so much more in the trenches. Guys did stuff on every single play you could never get away with these days.

I pulled a December 10, 1989 game up on YouTube and watched the whole thing because that was one of the most important games in rebuilding the foundation of Chiefs Kingdom. The Kansas City Chiefs defeated the Green Bay Packers 21–3. The funny thing about getting old is that you can be transported decades into the past—just like that. I watched the game and I forgot my old body; in my mind I was a 28-year-old football star again.

I wouldn't say that Green Bay was my best game, but I played well, rushing for 131 yards on 38—*38!*—carries with a touchdown, though I fumbled once because it was so damn cold. Although it's not my best game, it's one of my favorites because of what it said about our team during that era. It typified what we were all about: run the ball, impose our will, wear you down, hit you with some play-action passes, play great defense. It was the fulfillment of the vision Marty Schottenheimer expressed when he called me on the phone in the spring and told me in his confident, plainspoken way: "We're going to run the ball."

131

I'll set the scene for the game. There was a lot at stake. We came into the game with a record of 6–6–1, having won two in a row and then tied the game before. We were on a little hot streak that made us a surprising contender for the playoffs. We were starting to play Martyball and were playing the type of football that would make the Chiefs a playoff team six years straight starting in 1990. (Spoiler alert, though Chiefs fans know this: we got eliminated the next week when we lost at home against the San Diego Chargers and didn't make the playoffs in '89.)

The Packers were 8–5 and having a rebirth, too. Like us, they were a historic franchise that had stumbled on tough times, but they came into the game making a playoff push led by quarterback Don Majkowski and a wide-open offense ahead of its time and the opposite of ours. Nicknamed "The Majik Man," Majkowski and his Packers specialized in late-game comebacks. They'd been nicknamed "The Cardiac Pack" with four one-point victories—the last of which came the week before on a last-second field goal on the road against the Tampa Bay Buccaneers. Just like our fans, Green Bay fans were ecstatic to finally have a winner again, and the excitement grew as they continued to win. At the beginning of our game against them, NBC showed a clip of the Packers returning to the tiny airport in Green Bay, where they were greeted by 4,000 fans chanting "Go Pack Go!"

By then, my third year in the league, I had heard about all the history of Green Bay and Lambeau Field and was excited to see it for myself. But when I got there, I was disappointed and surprised that Green Bay was a tiny town in the middle of nowhere. For all that history, there was…nothing. It was humdrum, completely isolated, just some streets with suburban houses and nothing else, and I kept doing double-takes. *This was the place everyone was always talking about?*

The same goes for Lambeau Field. Nowadays, they have a brick façade to make it look like a classic, old-time building, but back then in 1989, it was a boring, utilitarian sports facility from the middle of the century, a scaled-up version of a high school stadium. Again, I was puzzled: *This was the great, historic stadium?*

But there was one aspect of Green Bay that exceeded my expectations: the cold. When the game started at 1:00 PM, it was 26 degrees—0 with the wind chill—with a 11-mph wind. We'd heard before the game there was an artic blast coming in, and it would get colder, and I remember standing out there, freezing my ass off, wondering how that was even possible. We'd been told what the temperature was going to be, but that didn't compute in my mind. As a guy from Nigeria who lived in California, zero degrees wasn't something I could conceptualize. I'd soon learn that standing outside for three hours in that that temperature is a special kind of misery.

The equipment guys gave me that heated thing you put around your waist, so you can thaw your hands. They gave me those little handwarmers to hold in my hand. I wore tights. I wore gloves inside my gloves. At the recommendation of some of my teammates, I rubbed up my body with Vaseline to preserve the heat. None of it did a thing. There's no way I could've been colder. I told myself to keep moving constantly while I was on the field. Between series I made a beeline for that hot air blower on the sideline, but there was lots of competition for spots in front of the several we had set up. They told us to stand some distance away, but I went right up against it. I didn't care if I burned my leg. Being lit on fire couldn't be more uncomfortable than the alternative. The field itself was heated underneath, so it was marshy. But the heating system didn't reach the sideline, so if you took a couple steps out of bounds, you were suddenly on an ice rink.

Everything about that game was difficult. Fortunately, weathering adversity was what Schottenheimer's Chiefs were all about.

*   *   *

When I watched this game on YouTube, the memories came flooding back. It's emotional because of the people. I was extremely close with these guys as a young man who was still a newcomer to the United States. These are the people I spent some of my best years with. These are the people who made me who I am.

While watching I appreciated again our great defense, who halted the Green Bay Packers on their first drive thanks to an Albert Lewis sack off a blitz. I watched Marty Schottenheimer walk a few steps out on the field, clapping, shaking hands with the guys individually, swatting them on their butts, looking them in the eye and saying, "Good job."

That was Schottenheimer in a nutshell. He was always involved in every detail, always hands-on, and always made the time to address every player as an individual. That was a big difference I noticed immediately from Frank Gansz, who was a nice guy, but the job seemed too big for him. Schottenheimer was aware of every detail of every player's responsibility.

Our first offensive play of the game was a run to me. Even that play showed Schottenheimer's influence: I got hit in the backfield, but I kept my legs moving and I wound up breaking the tackle and gaining a few yards when I should've lost a few. That was something Schottenheimer had the time and energy to drill into me every day in practice since training camp: "Keep your legs moving." I can still hear him saying that. It was one of the many things that wasn't intuitive to me but became second nature the more Schottenheimer said them and the more I focused on them in practice. By the latter part of the '89 season, I was in the habit of keeping my legs moving and turning negative plays into positive ones. It's a simple directive, but that's what made Schottenheimer such a great coach. He didn't overcomplicate things; he just knew exactly which simple things to emphasize. He didn't have a big ego and didn't need to think of himself as a guru or genius. Rather, he was a teacher who broke things down to their simple components. That was something I really embraced as a track guy.

Another thing Schottenheimer would keep repeating in his speeches to the team was "One play at a time." The way he'd say it, it was as if he was talking about something deep and philosophical, which he was. Our team took it to heart as a rallying cry, and as I've gotten older, I realize how much I apply it to everything. Take pride in every moment. Every little thing is a reflection of you, and the big things are just the accumulation of little things. (Another of my favorite Schottenheimer expressions was "Hang in there like an old sack of balls." Schottenheimer was a serious guy, but he had a sharp wit and was naturally funny.)

Schottenheimer was straightforward, but he was very smart and even erudite. He'd been an English major in college, and his speeches were very eloquent and inspirational. He made us feel like we were a part of something important and valuable and that being a Kansas City Chief was a meaningful thing. That wasn't a feeling we'd had during my first two years in the league.

And yet, I didn't get to know him as a person all that much during my career. It was obvious that we respected each other and were fond of each other, but our relationship was purely professional; we didn't talk about our families or other topics. When I retired, we became much closer, and I told him I regretted that we hadn't become closer when we worked together. His reply showed how perceptive he was about people. He said there were a lot of guys on the team he needed to motivate, to play psychologist with, but I wasn't one of them. He said he knew how self-motivated I was and that he could give me instructions and trust me to do my best to follow them. He said he left me alone because he trusted me.

Years later, I was devastated to learn he was suffering from Alzheimer's disease—likely resulting from his career in football, when he'd played for six years in the pros as a linebacker, having collisions on every play for years. After his diagnosis I saw him at an early stage of the disease in Palm Springs, California, and I honestly didn't notice anything different. He seemed fine, and I held out hope that the disease wouldn't take its course. But two years later, I heard he was suffering, and it broke my heart. It was so unfair: here was a man who was so full of energy and intelligence, a guy who had so much love for his players and passion for them as human beings, and the disease was slowly taking all that away from him, stripping him of all his great qualities while he was still alive. He was one of the most capable people I'd ever been around, and the thought of him being debilitated was crushing.

When he died, it hit me like a family member dying. We'd become close as adults and friends, and he had known me since my youth and become a father figure to me. I couldn't get past the idea that I'd never see him again, that this was it. I thought about his wife Pat, who was such a solid, good person in exactly the same way Marty was. I thought about their family and what a terrible loss it was for them.

It was a terrible loss for a lot of people. Schottenheimer touched so many lives. In fact, one of the coaches he'd mentored was across the sideline from us that day in Green Bay. Packers head coach Lindy Infante had been

Schottenheimer's offensive coordinator with the Cleveland Browns. Other branches of his coaching tree included four Super Bowl champions—Bruce Arians, Tony Dungy, Bill Cowher, and Mike McCarthy—each of whom will tell you how much Schottenheimer meant to them.

I owe my career to him, too. If he hadn't called me before the 1989 season and told me, "Prepare yourself to run the ball," I would've been forgotten about a long time ago. If not for Schottenheimer, there wouldn't have been a reawakening of Chiefs Kingdom.

That all started in 1989. And the excitement about what Schottenheimer and us were building really got going during that game in Green Bay.

We didn't score on our first drive, but on our second drive, early in the second quarter, we did. Our quarterback, Steve DeBerg, hit a play-action pass to move us downfield. Then from our 11-yard-line, DeBerg threw a touchdown pass to our tight end, Jonathan Hayes, which was set up by a fake to me.

Play-faking was the reason DeBerg had grabbed hold of the starting quarterback job by the 11th game of the '89 season and didn't let go of it. DeBerg was the best I'd ever see do it; he and I worked very well as a tandem. DeBerg would reach the ball all the way into my stomach and then pull it out at the last moment. With play-faking you have to really sell it—you can't just go through the motions—and both of us knew that and worked to sell every aspect of it. The difference between success and failure resides in the littlest things, as Schottenheimer constantly preached to us.

DeBerg had been benched twice that year. First for Ron Jaworski, then for Steve Pelluer, for whom we traded two picks and then soon after inserted into the starting lineup. DeBerg's issue had been turnovers, which Schottenheimer hated even more than most coaches, and over a three-week stretch, DeBerg committed nine of them. But Jaworski got hurt, and then Pelluer did, and DeBerg was back as our starter with a new nickname: Freddy Krueger. Like the horror movie villain, DeBerg kept coming back from the dead. DeBerg was 35 by then; he'd been around the league at a bunch of stops but had always lost his starting job to a big-name quarterback. With the San Francisco 49ers, he'd lost his job to Joe Montana. With the Denver Broncos, he'd lost his job to John Elway. With the Tampa Bay Buccaneers, he'd lost his job when they drafted Vinny Testaverde first overall.

When he came to Kansas City, it was obvious that DeBerg saw it as his last, best shot to lead a team, and he was on a mission. Play-faking was a key component of our offense, and DeBerg worked tirelessly at it until he perfected it. In meetings DeBerg was serious and intense; he wanted to get it right. I remember once noticing how DeBerg's demeanor was different from Jaworski's. Jaworski was at the tail end of a very successful career, during which he'd made a Pro Bowl with the Philadelphia Eagles and taken them to a Super Bowl and multiple playoff appearances. He was relaxed, enjoying his twilight years. DeBerg was motivated by desperation to have some success as a starting quarterback before it was all over.

He fit right in with what our team was all about. We were a running team, and DeBerg was a master of play-action fakes. We were a team who wasn't highly regarded coming into the season just like DeBerg. We were a team that was willing to work its ass off to have some success just like DeBerg was. Schottenheimer and DeBerg would watch game film together every Friday, and DeBerg absorbed everything that Schottenheimer pointed out. It showed how hands-on Schottenheimer was and it showed DeBerg's capacity for work.

DeBerg took the starting job and ran with it in '89, and the Green Bay game was his best of the year. He completed 15-of-19 passes for 203 yards and two touchdowns. Toward the end of the fourth quarter, he was named the Budweiser Player of the Game. NBC showed that red Budweiser graphic around one of his great plays.

In 1989 the Chiefs found an identity. And a quarterback.

*   *   *

Two drives after our first score, still in the second quarter, Steve DeBerg took us deep into Green Bay Packers territory again. From that point it was my turn. From the 3-yard line, I followed a pulling guard to the right, ran through an arm tackle, and fell forward into the end zone, giving us a 14–3 lead.

I was a big, fast guy obviously, but there's more to running through contact than being big and fast. What's important is the little moment of mental preparation for a collision, the smallest flash in your consciousness. You lower your shoulder, you brace for impact, you tell yourself to go as hard as possible. For me simple physics dictated that the defender would likely get the worst of it. That confidence gave me that extra oomph, and I knew if I brought that *oomph*, I'd fall forward, and the other guy would fall backward.

I had to train myself to do that. I'm not a violent person, so it's not in my nature to relish that violent contact, to seek out the collision. But I am someone who wants to do a good job, which means I was able to train my body to do what it needed to do to get the job done.

I scored against the Packers and stood up in the endzone. We're winning by 11 points in a notoriously tough environment with just over one minute remaining in the first half. My teammates ran over to congratulate me, slapping me on my back, my ass, and my helmet. The crowd was silent, but I heard my teammates' voices perfectly. That's the sound of a job well done.

There was only about a minute left in the half, but we weren't done. On a Don Majkowski pass attempt, Neil Smith beat the blocker across from him and then used his seven-foot wingspan to swat the ball out of Majkowski's hand. Then, he recovered the fumble himself deep in our territory. That was Smith, an athletic freak who made plays nobody else could.

On our ensuing drive in the final seconds of the half, DeBerg fired a 12-yard touchdown pass to Emile Harry on a square-in to give us a 21–3 lead. It was a perfect pass in a tight window—more evidence that it was DeBerg's time.

And that was all the scoring for the game. We ran out the clock for the rest of the game. Most of my yardage came in the second half, though I fumbled as well. Safety Chuck Cecil, who was known for his ferocious, headfirst hits, made a missile of himself and flew toward me, jarring the ball loose with his helmet. I had no feel for the ball because of how cold it was. But overall, it was a good game for me, and I was happy with the way I did my job.

I enjoyed watching our defense. We're talking about some of the best players in Chiefs history. Smith, who forced the fumble on Majkowski, was drafted No. 2 overall in 1988, the year before but didn't produce all that much his rookie year, notching just 2.5 sacks. But he started to put it together by '89 and eventually would become one of the best defensive players in the league, making six Pro Bowls from the left defensive end spot.

Smith worked hard to improve and he was very close with outside linebacker Derrick Thomas, who lined up on the opposite side from Smith and in my opinion was the best pass rusher in the history of the league. Those guys gave us a huge advantage on defense. Nobody had that kind of edge-rushing talent on both sides. The two of them were extremely gifted athletically, but what made them so special was their work ethic. Off the field, they would constantly study film and talk about pass rushing moves and all the little things edge rushers could do to gain an edge.

I've never seen a more talented football player than Thomas. The funny thing about Thomas was that he hated practice. Every week Marty Schottenheimer would yell at him because his head was somewhere else. But come Sunday he was electric, and nobody played with more intensity. It was as if he'd been storing up all that energy all week. On Sundays he was moving at a different speed than anyone else.

Thomas was a superstar from the moment he hit the field. In 1989 he made the Pro Bowl and was named the AP Defensive Rookie of the Year. He gave our team some star power and swagger; he was the final piece of the puzzle for our already very good defense to become dominant. His signature moment came a year later in a game against the Seattle Seahawks, when he had seven sacks, setting an NFL record that still stands. What a lot of people don't remember is that Thomas actually had *nine* sacks that day, but two came on plays that were called back because of a defensive penalty. That's how good Thomas was.

I noticed while watching the YouTube video of the Packers game that Thomas was on special teams, which is something you'd never see in today's game but shows how much Schottenheimer felt he needed to get Thomas onto the field. Thomas was like a time bomb. You knew he'd make something happen at some point, but you weren't sure when. You just wanted to give him as many opportunities as possible to make that happen.

And in Green Bay, even though he didn't have a sack, he made a huge play in the third quarter, when the Packers got a big gain into our territory that could have given them a foothold back into the game. But the play was nullified. Badly beaten off the edge by Thomas' quickness, the Packers left tackle got called for a holding penalty, which basically killed their drive. The Packers never threatened again.

I got to know Thomas pretty well his rookie year because we sometimes roomed together on the road. He was a guy with a big heart who was very involved in charity work. He founded his Third and Long Foundation in 1990 with a mission of improving literacy and education among low-income kids in the Kansas City area. Every Saturday, Thomas would read to kids at local libraries. The fact that our best player was also a great human being did so much to bond our team with our city. The foundation still exists more than two decades after Thomas' death. Smith and I are both board members.

Thomas' death in 2000—16 days after a car crash that left him para-lyzed—was the most shocking thing I've ever experienced. It's still shock-ing to me all these years later because I thought the guy was indestructible. I remember that day like it was yesterday. I was in California, watching *SportsCenter* in the morning when a breaking news bulletin came on: Thomas had been rushing to the airport in Kansas City to fly to St. Louis to see the St. Louis Rams and Tampa Bay Buccaneers play the NFC Championship Game and he'd been in a horrible crash caused by the snow and ice. Thomas wasn't wearing a seatbelt, and neither was his friend, Michael Tellis, who was thrown from the vehicle and pronounced dead at the scene. Thomas, who was also thrown from the car, severely hurt his spine and broke three vertebrae. He vowed he would walk again, and I didn't doubt he would.

Thomas was transferred to a hospital in Miami, and I booked a ticket to visit him. Shortly before I was going to leave for the airport to see him, I saw another breaking news alert on *SportsCenter*: Thomas had died from a massive blood clot. He was 33.

I cried on the spot, and the pain lingers to this day. Whenever I get to together with former teammates, there's never a time when we don't talk about Thomas. But his foundation lives on and so does his community work and the lives he touched. After Thomas died, the Chiefs' head coach at the time, Gunther Cunningham, told *The New York Times*, "I looked at Derrick Thomas as one of the finest people I've ever been around and a friend. Derrick will hang over this stadium forever."

That's all true, but it's even more than that. Thomas will hang over the Kansas City area forever.

*   *   *

The additions of Neil Smith and Derrick Thomas in back-to-back drafts gave us a star-studded defensive front to match our secondary, which had already been the best in the league but had never gotten proper recognition before 1989 because our team hadn't been successful.

Albert Lewis was the best cover corner in the league, a 6'2", long-limbed, very fast, very athletic player. Lewis was like Thomas: he was such a superior athlete the coaches devised ways to get him onto the field and make plays. His blitz early in the Green Bay game was one example. So were the many punts he blocked during his career, when he'd come off the edge like a swooping eagle. Lewis was such a dynamic force on the field, but off the field, he was quiet.

But his fellow cornerback did plenty of talking for the both of them. Kevin Ross from just outside of Philadelphia had an East Coast mouth and swagger that he backed up on the field. Ross and Lewis were the best cornerback tandem in the league in that era and maybe the best of all time. We called him "Rock." He was small in stature—he was listed at 5'9", and that was generous—but he'd hit you as hard as a rock. He was also a smart player and nowadays he's the cornerbacks coach with the Tampa Bay Buccaneers. The guy who hired him was someone on our coaching staff in 1989: Bruce Arians, who knew Ross from way back when he'd coached him at Temple University.

Our free safety, Deron Cherry, was the smartest football player I've ever been around: The guy had an amazing knack for anticipating where the ball was going, which is how he made six Pro Bowls and intercepted 50 passes in his career. His partner at the safety position, Lloyd Burruss, had a quiet personality but was an intimidating hitter, one of those strong safeties who came up and hit like a linebacker.

I can't talk about the defense without mentioning our run stuffers up front. Bill Maas, a defensive tackle who made two Pro Bowls, was incredibly serious on the field and became a leader because of his intensity. Next to him was Dan Saleaumua, who made a Pro Bowl and was as happy-go-lucky as Maas was serious. Saleaumua would crack jokes in practice, between plays, and right up until his hand was in the dirt—and then he'd get serious, and it was impossible to block him because he was a bowling ball-shaped, 305-pound man.

Our defense was loaded with stars. (Smith, Thomas, and most of our secondary from that Packers game are now members of the Chiefs Hall of Honor.) As a Schottenheimer-coached team, we played through our defense, trying to control the clock on offense so we could keep those guys fresh and enable

My grandfather, Chief Jacob Aguolu, wears traditional attire. (*Christian Okoye*)

My parents, Benedict and Cecilia Okoye, celebrate their wedding day. (*Christian Okoye*)

My mother, Cecilia, as a young woman. (*Christian Okoye*)

My mother (left) stands with her younger sister, Vicky. (*Christian Okoye*)

I hang out with my siblings. Top row: me, Obiageli, Chikwelu and bottom row: Loretta, Stanislaus, Benedeth, Emmanuel. (*Christian Okoye*)

My father and I attend the Kansas City Chiefs banquet, in which I won the Mack Lee Hill Award for top rookie on the team. (*Christian Okoye*)

I throw the discus, the skill that brought me to America, in 1982.

I pose in my Azusa Pacific track gear in 1986.

Discus throwers are big guys. Here I am—the smallest of the bunch—throwing the discus with my fellow competitors.

I take a handoff during my breakout year in 1985, when I had 1,355 yards in just nine games for Azusa Pacific.

I run the ball in 1986, when I led the NAIA with 1,680 yards and 21 touchdowns and earned All-American honors.

During my rookie year in 1987, I run for a chunk of my team-high 58 rushing yards in a 16–9 loss to the New York Jets. (*AP Images*)

Bruce Arians talks to me as I stand next to my good friend Derrick Thomas, who I miss dearly, before a game against the Denver Broncos in 1989. (*AP Images*)

In a victory that would forever change things in Chiefs Kingdom, I rush for some of my game-high 131 yards on 38 carries against the Green Bay Packers—in the frigid weather of Lambeau Field in 1989. (*AP Images*)

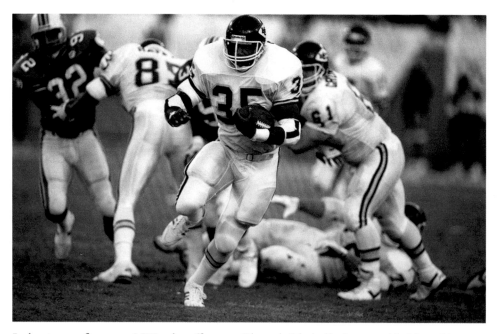

I play in my first ever NFL playoff game. Though I led all players with 83 rushing yards, we lost 17–16 to the Miami Dolphins in January of 1991. (*AP Images*)

I appear in a popular Costacos Brothers poster, which spoofed my nickname and the film, *A Nightmare on Elm Street*. (*Christian Okoye*)

After the Kansas City Chiefs won Super Bowl LIV, owner Clark Hunt graciously gave me and my fellow Chiefs Ambassadors a Super Bowl ring. (*Christian Okoye*)

I receive induction into the NAIA Hall of Fame in 1992.

Upon the Chiefs landing in Arizona for Super Bowl LVII, I take a selfie with Patrick Mahomes and Travis Kelce. (*AP Images*)

them to do their thing. The Green Bay game was a great example of this. We had the ball for 37 minutes; the Packers had it for 23. To control the clock, you needed to make first downs on the ground, and that's where I came in.

With a big lead in the second half, we decided to run the ball. The first five plays of the second half, I got the ball. It was a statement: we knew that they knew it was coming and we didn't care. In fact, we liked it. It made the accomplishment of stacking up first downs that much more rewarding. As Schottenheimer always said about our basic off-tackle play: "The defense knows it's coming, even the fans know it's coming, but still nobody can stop us."

That's how the second half played out. We chewed up clock, we wore them down, we kept our defense fresh to shut their offense down, and we kept the score exactly as it was at halftime, winning 21–3. (We even overcame a couple of turnovers, including my fumble.)

It's a crazy thing to watch tape of yourself as a younger man playing such a violent sport. In one part of my mind, I'm still 28 and I think I can still do all the things I'm watching myself do. But in another part of my mind, I'm blown away that I ever played such a crazy game to begin with. Another observation from watching that game: there's never been a running back who looked anything like me on the field, particularly the guys nowadays, who are short and shifty and hardly wear pads.

I was huge, and my pads made me look bigger. The fiberglass addition to my shoulder pads—designed to prevent my neck from snapping back— gave me my signature look. It was complemented by the facemask I wore with the one bar coming down, which always made me look like I was leaning forward, looming, and menacing. You never see guys wearing that facemask anymore, but I always felt it protected my eyes, and when I watch myself on tape, it looks right. I wore every pad that was available—knee pads, thigh pads, hip pads—and the biggest, thickest version of each. Some guys make a macho thing out of not wearing heavy pads, but I never felt I had anything to prove. In fact, I always felt looking as big as possible was intimidating to the other team, who didn't want to tackle someone who looked like me running right at them.

So on YouTube, I watched that 28-year-old me chewing up the clock in Green Bay. I watched our offensive linemen get a spring in their step when we called running play after running play. I watched the body language of the defenders, those little signs of giving up that show that they're only human, and nobody wants to be out there in the zero-degree wind chill, exhausted, on a marshy field, and being forced to tackle a 265-pound guy running at them over and over again.

We kicked the Packers' ass. It was a great win, the best of the season. Toward the end of the game, the Packers fans chanted "Go Pack Go" in appreciation of their team, an acknowledgement that it still had been a great year despite their loss. The Packers had a terrific fanbase that deserved a winner. The same was true of our fans.

It was our third win in a row. Counting our tie at the Cleveland Browns a few weeks before, we hadn't lost a game in our last four games. That was a big deal for a team that had gotten so used to losing. It showed how much Schottenheimer had turned our mentality around. Going forward, as long as Schottenheimer was there, the Chiefs would be winners.

12

PLAYOFFS AT LAST

When I think of 1990, I don't think about a football season. I think about the worst thing that ever happened to me. After my wife Lauren got pregnant, we named our son Michael Christian Okoye. For the next few months, I daydreamed about being a dad and what I would do with him. I told myself I'd learn how to play baseball because Michael would be an American boy who loved baseball. Lauren and I went shopping; we got him the little clothes and little shoes.

Lauren was about eight months pregnant when she noticed the baby wasn't moving around nearly as much as he had been. Feeling the baby move had been my favorite part; I used to love when Lauren would lie down, and we'd put our hands on her belly and feel our little guy moving and kicking. But he suddenly was moving less and less. We booked an appointment with our doctor. It so happened on that day that our regular obstetrician wasn't there, so we saw another doctor from the practice. He told us the baby was probably fine, but if the baby's movement didn't pick up after a few days, we should come in again.

On July 12, 1990, the baby wasn't moving at all. We called the doctor's office. They told us to immediately go to the hospital, where Lauren had an emergency C-section. They didn't let me in the room. I was standing outside for about an hour and a half, but it seemed like much longer. Finally, the doctor came out: the baby was alive, but he wasn't breathing well, and they were trying to get him to breathe better. The doctor went back in, and I was alone again and completely powerless. It seemed like days passed, but I'm told it was only 23 minutes later when the doctor came out and said my son had died. Perinatal asphyxia. His lungs hadn't been getting enough oxygen for weeks, and after he came out of the womb, he couldn't survive.

My first feeling was numbness. It was like I was standing outside myself. My greatest fear had actually just happened. It didn't quite feel real.

When it sunk in, sadness overwhelmed me. For a long time, Lauren and I just cried and held each other in that hospital bed. I felt terrible for her: *she* had carried this baby. She had just been cut open for the C-section. I was devastated emotionally, but she was destroyed in every way possible after carrying Michael for nearly nine months. As a man I still can't fully grasp what she must have been going through.

After the sadness came anger. I saw smiling couples leaving the hospital with their perfect healthy babies. I was surrounded by people having the best moments of their lives and I was having the worst. It felt like a nightmare. I kept asking over and over, *Why did this happen to me? What did I do to deserve this?*

Decades later, all those feelings have faded into the background, but they're still with me. I visit Michael's grave and place flowers by his headstone. Lauren and I are now divorced, but I'll snap a photo of the flowers by Michael's grave and send it to her. We're not together, but we're forever united in grief. The only people who understand our sadness about Michael are each other. Then my mind wanders, and I start imagining he's alive, a man in his 30s now. What kind of a man is Michael? Which sports is he into? Is he a football fan? Does he like going to Kansas City Chiefs games with me? What's it like when I take him to Chiefs games?

*   *   *

For a stretch of time after Michael's death, I needed to be with Lauren. Training camp was around the corner, but football was the furthest thing from my mind. I called the Kansas City Chiefs and told somebody at the office what had happened. General manager Carl Peterson was the first person to call me back. "Take your time. Take care of your family. Don't come back until you're ready," he said. I was never more thankful than in that moment that I was a Chief.

Several weeks went by. My sister Loretta visited from Nigeria and she helped me support Lauren. Training camp was well underway when Lauren told me that it was time. She felt stronger. Life had to move on. So I went back to camp.

When I got there, Peterson told me that they'd fielded constant questions about me, but they didn't tell reporters anything—only that I was dealing with some personal things and that they were supporting me in my absence. I preferred it that way; I didn't want anyone asking me about Michael, preferring to keep my privacy. But Peterson told me there'd been a media member who'd been popping off about why I wasn't in camp, making up rumors that I was holding out for more money and painting me as a bad teammate. Peterson shut that down. He banned the guy from our facility. I don't even remember the guy's name.

To my recollection the media never mentioned my son's passing, and I'm forever grateful to Peterson for how he handled the whole situation. The fact that Peterson, Marty Schottenheimer, and everyone else with the Chiefs handled it the way they did says a lot about them. This was 1990;

the world has changed a lot since then. They didn't have to do that, but they did because they were good people.

It's fair to say that Peterson wasn't the most popular guy in the Chiefs' locker room at the time. As the GM he sat across the negotiating table from the players, and a natural antagonism resulted. But he's a good man, and now that we're both older, I consider him a friend. Chiefs fans should be as grateful to him as I am. It was Peterson, along with Schottenheimer, who engineered the rebirth of Chiefs Kingdom.

One of the smartest moves Peterson made was signing Barry Word before the 1990 season. Word was talented but had gone through some troubles at the beginning of his career. But by the time I met him, that was all in the past. The guy I knew was a total professional and a great person who became my close friend.

Actually, Word—along with Jonathan Hayes and Steve DeBerg—is one of the Chiefs I remain closest to in the present day. He lives across the country in Virginia, so we seldom see each other aside from at Chiefs-related events in Kansas City, but we talk on the phone all the time. Word is a chill guy, a good-natured person who's easy to talk to. When he came to the Chiefs in 1990, everyone thought we'd be enemies competing for carries from the running back position, but we got along great from Day One. I actually think Word extended my career for a few years by taking the pressure off me. I had 370 carries in 1989. There's no way I could've done another year of that.

In 1990 we needed Word because I was compromised in many ways. The first is the most obvious one: the shock and grief from my baby's death was still fresh. Going out there every day felt like playing football with an open wound. But I was also dealing with mounting physical injuries, which caused near constant pain. The offseason prior to the '90 season, I'd undergone surgery to repair my right shoulder after I'd separated it the year before—the doctors stapled my ligament to the bone—and the rehab was painful and tedious. My knees were also in bad shape; I'd partially torn my right PCL the year before and missed just one game but otherwise played through it. Both knees would continue to deteriorate for the rest of my career and beyond. Then, toward the end of the '90 season, I separated my *left* shoulder, causing me to miss several games.

By that point, I was addicted to a narcotic painkiller called indomethacin. I took a pill every day during the season and during the offseason because the pain never stopped, though it was harder because doctors wouldn't give it to me in the offseason. I needed it if I was going to keep playing the sport because injuries never really go away in football; they just heal enough so you can play with them. For three hours on Sundays, the indomethacin worked like magic. But after games the pills would wear off, and the pain would come back in full force, and I'd realize that one way or another there's no escaping that football is pain, and the toll to this brutal game must be paid. The injuries I was fighting—plus everything I was dealing with emotionally—impacted my preparation. The only time I felt good was after I took those pills, and the adrenaline of the game briefly made me forget everything. Every other moment that season was a physical, mental, and emotional struggle.

Consequently, 1990 was a down season for me. I rushed for just 805 yards after recording 1,480 the year before. As the year went on, Word cut into my carries and put together a great season, rushing for 1,015 yards on 5.0 yards per carry. By the time the playoffs rolled around, I'd missed several games with my separated shoulder, and Word was the starter.

And I was happy for him—and happy for our team. Sure, a part of me always worried about my job security, and a part of me thought, *Uh oh, they don't need me anymore.* But what happened with my son had changed my mindset. I wasn't sweating the small stuff like which guy was starting and how many carries we were getting. Ever since I was a kid, growing up with a brutal civil war raging outside my door, I'd always been able to make the best of situations, to look on the bright side, so to speak. And there was a huge bright side to Word's emergence. It took the pressure off me. The team could succeed even if I wasn't at my best.

And succeed we did. We went 11–5, and our 11 wins were the most for a Chiefs team since the Super Bowl season of 1969. It had been a long down period for the Chiefs, but in '90 we made the playoffs for the first time since 1986 and only the third time since that '69 season. We finished second in the division to the Los Angeles Raiders, who finished 12–4, but we beat them in both meetings and felt we were the better team. Our defense forced more turnovers than any team in the league, and our offense had the second fewest turnovers. We sacked the quarterback a league-high 60 times, including 20 by Derrick Thomas.

But the biggest reason for our success in 1990 was something nobody saw coming: DeBerg. At the age of 36, he suddenly became one of the best quarterbacks in the league. He had the NFL's third best quarterback rating and led us to the sixth most points scored in the league, along with the seventh most yards.

Early in the season before, the coaches had been desperate to move on from him because of how many interceptions he was throwing at the beginning of the season. In 1990 he was the exact opposite. In 444 pass attempts, DeBerg threw just four interceptions. His 0.9 interception percentage was the best by an NFL quarterback that year, and during a stretch that season, he went 233 consecutive pass attempts without an interception. (I don't think people fully appreciate how remarkable this is. Think about what it says about a quarterback to transform himself so completely at that age.)

DeBerg was such a competitor. He didn't have the strongest arm in the league, but what he had were smarts and toughness. An example of those smarts came when we were playing the Raiders in Los Angeles late in the '90 season. We'd already beaten them at home a few weeks earlier, and the winner would get the inside track to the division title. We were up by three in the fourth quarter, needing a touchdown to take control of the game. DeBerg took matters into his own hands. He brilliantly adjusted his cadence, causing the Raiders to jump offside *four* times on a single drive, which set up a touchdown pass. (We won the game, but unfortunately the Raiders won their remaining slate to take the division.)

He also had toughness. Chiefs fans of a certain age will remember the huge cast DeBerg had on his left pinkie finger and ring finger. He'd broken it against the Houston Oilers, but it was more severe than just broken fingers. It was pulverized, smashed to bits, and DeBerg needed to have surgery, where doctors stabilized the finger by implanting a plastic pin, which stuck out about an inch past his fingertip, into his finger. It was crazy and disgusting, and the doctors covered it up with a huge cast. How he came back to play against the San Diego Chargers the next week I have no idea, but DeBerg was at his best, completing his first eight passes and leading us to a 24–21 win that clinched a playoff berth. To see a quarterback playing through a gruesome injury is inspiring. To see him be at his best is the type of effort that lifts an entire team and makes his teammates love him. And everyone on those Chiefs teams loved DeBerg.

Decades after we played together, he's still a close friend of mine. He is just such a positive guy, the type of person who makes you feel better about yourself and everything else. He's one of my closest friends, and I frequently visit him in Tampa, where he goes out on his boat and fishes, and I go out on his boat and just sit in the sun. He is fiercely loyal, the type of friend I have no doubt will do anything for me just like I'll do the same for him. We forged that bond in the Chiefs' huddle and we're still that close.

It was around 2011 when I went to visit him at his place in Tampa, where he still lives. We had a few drinks, and at a certain point, he said, "Here, let me show you something."

We went to a room where he kept all his memorabilia, trophies, and keepsakes, including that huge cast he wore on his hand at the end of the '90 season. He said, "Do you remember this?"

I said I did and I asked him for a sharpie. He found one and gave it to me, and I signed the cast: "To Steve, Christian Okoye. Thank you."

He smiled, looked at the cast, and said sarcastically, "*Thank you?* No, thank *you* for missing that block and getting my pinkie broken."

According to DeBerg, on the play he broke that finger, I'd missed a block on one side, and another defender got loose on the other side. The two defenders converged on DeBerg, and his finger got smashed in between their helmets. I have no recollection of the play, but I'll take his word for it. After all, it was his finger, not mine.

*   *   *

Thanks to Steve DeBerg's courage, the 1990 Kansas City Chiefs were heading to the playoffs—my first trip to the postseason in my four years in the league to that point. My shoulder healed up enough, and I took enough indomethacin that I was able to play. This was the playoffs, and I needed to be there for my team. We were off to Miami to play the Dolphins, who under Don Shula were always one of the best teams in the league. To get our bodies acclimated to the heat and humidity, Marty Schottenheimer had us go to Vero Beach, Florida, to practice that week. I loved it; I'd never gotten used to the winters in the Midwest and welcomed any chance to get away.

As expected, our game against the Dolphins was physical and punishing. It was the type of game in which my team was counting on me to play well. Thankfully, I felt as good as I had all season. Part of it was the fresh start of the postseason, where everybody is 0–0. Part of it was the warm weather, which reawakened my body. And part of it is that I always had success against the Dolphins because I was always very comfortable running against a 3-4 defense. Facing that 3-4 scheme, I developed a knack for reading the defensive end on the play side. Usually, our blockers would get a good enough block on that defensive end that I'd run inside of him, and if he was distracted by our blockers at all, he could only attempt to arm tackle me, which just wasn't going to work. But if that defensive end beat his blocker to the inside, I'd quickly read that and just bounce it outside of him. After that sometimes I'd cut it up inside of the outside linebacker. Sometimes I'd bounce it toward the sideline, and I was fast enough to beat defenders to the corner when I did. In a 3-4 defense, the second level of defenders were the inside linebackers, but they lined up four to five yards off the line of scrimmage. I lined up 7.5 yards into the backfield and was bigger than almost all of them. In that collision I had the advantage.

So, against the Dolphins, I had a good game, rushing for 83 yards on 13 carries. And our defense was putting on a show. Through 42 minutes the Dolphins hadn't advanced past our 40 yard-line, and we led 16–3. But then Dan Marino went to work, leading his team to two touchdown drives, putting the Dolphins up 17–16. It was something to watch. Even when you're a player in the NFL, where everyone's an incredible athlete, certain guys set themselves apart and make their peers look on them with awe. Marino was one of those guys; his quick, fluid release was a thing of beauty, just a sight to behold for anyone who's into athletics of any kind. I remember the way the ball would zip through the air. He threw such a tight, perfect spiral. You could swear you could hear it whistle.

Down by one point, we had a little more than three minutes to drive ourselves into field-goal range. All year long we'd shown the ability to pick ourselves up off the mat and we did it again in Miami. DeBerg completed a 20-yard pass to Stephone Paige, and I took a stretch play off the left side for 26 yards down to the Miami 26-yard line. At that point, we had basically done what we had to do: we'd set up a 43-yard field goal for our kicker, Nick Lowery, who at the time had the most accurate kicking percentage in the history of the NFL and is a member of the Chiefs Hall of Honor. Forty-three yards was in Lowery's range. His longest field goal of the year was 48 yards.

We wanted to chew up some more clock to get closer and we knew the Dolphins defense was exhausted. So we ran the same play the next time, and I cut it up in the middle, running for 12 yards, which would've made Lowery's attempt a chip shot and would've allowed us to run the clock out, basically sealing the game. But then I saw the yellow flag back toward the line of scrimmage. Anyone who has ever watched football knows what that means. It was a holding penalty on our rookie guard, Dave Szott, a good player and a good guy, that pushed us back to the 38-yard line.

Over the next three plays, we managed just three yards. Lowery came out for a 52-yard field goal. His kick was perfectly accurate but inches short. It was one of the most crushing defeats in the history of the Chiefs' franchise, certainly the worst loss in my career. We could've done some damage in the playoffs—and I had only just gotten going.

But a part of me was relieved it was over. It had been an exhausting year—physically and emotionally. I needed to heal up my body and I needed to get back to my regular training in time for the '91 season. I needed to get my head straight after pushing myself through a season after Michael's death. Most importantly, I needed to be with Lauren. By that point she was pregnant again.

I healed, I trained, and by the summer, my body felt ready for the '91 season. Lauren and I learned we were having a girl. But about six months into her pregnancy, there was a potential problem: the baby's umbilical cord was wrapped around her neck several times. The baby was doing fine, but this was cause for concern. For the next couple of months, it seemed like we were constantly in the doctor's office. It got to the point where we went every day, which meant that every day we worried that the baby would be in distress. Every day the doctor reassured us the baby was fine. Every day we worried and prayed.

Finally, in late August, a little before Lauren was due, the doctor said it was the safest move to take the baby out. We scheduled the C-section, and this time I was in the room. This time, the baby was crying, which meant everything was okay. I looked up at the doctors and the nurses just to make sure, and they were all smiling.

It had been just 13 months ago when I'd seen all those smiling parents in the hospital. Now I was one of those smiling parents. Tiana Okoye was born on August 26, 1991. Along with the birth of my two other children years later, Tiana's birth was the happiest moment of my life. In 13 months I'd gone from the worst moment of my life to the best.

13

1991 AND RAUCOUS
ARROWHEAD

Going into the 1991 season, I had a beautiful, healthy baby. Physically, I was feeling as good as I ever would again, though I wasn't close to being 100 percent. I was motivated to reassert myself as a premier running back. I was on a team with Super Bowl aspirations. When I got to training camp, I had a feeling that I was in for a good year.

And I was. I rushed for 1,031 yards, averaging 4.6 per attempt, and made the Pro Bowl. I was 30 years old, and my body was obviously wearing down, but my knowledge of the game made up for it. That's something I've thought about a lot with some regret. It took me many years to learn the sport and catch up to my American peers who grew up playing football. By the time I knew what I was doing out there, my body was practically shot.

But in '91 I still had something left in the tank—and I proved that when I rushed for 143 yards in our first game of the season, and we defeated the Atlanta Falcons 14–3. But after that we were inconsistent as a team. We dropped our next two games and won the two after that, setting up a *Monday Night Football* game in Week Six against the Buffalo Bills, the defending AFC Champions. We were 3–2; they were 5–0—and they talked a lot of shit in the media that week. Someone—and I forget the player's name—had said that they had marked the Kansas City Chiefs game as a win when they looked at the schedule. Generally, they came across as having no respect for us. They made it clear they didn't consider us on their level, that we weren't ready for primetime.

It turned out we were ready—and so were our fans. It was the Chiefs' first *Monday Night Football* game since 1983, and hours before the game, when I pulled into the Arrowhead Stadium parking lot, I saw a haze of smoke from the tailgate party grills and smelled that delicious barbecue smell. The parking lot was packed.

The Bills never had a chance. We beat them 33–6. It was just as Marty Schottenheimer had imagined his football team. We sacked Jim Kelly six times and forced five turnovers. (Derrick Thomas had four of those sacks.) Harvey Williams and I both rushed for more than 100 yards, and I scored two touchdowns, punctuating one of them by flexing my arms like body-builder and yelling at the top of my lungs. (Usually, my move was just to hand the ball to the ref, but I was excited.) We held the ball for 44 minutes; they held it for 16.

And Arrowhead rocked. It rocked louder than I'd ever heard a stadium rock. The days of the listless, sparse crowds and those wide-open patches of red seats were a distant memory. In the coming years, Arrowhead would develop the reputation as the loudest stadium in the league with the most enthusiastic fans—fans who made it their business to be a part of the game. That night Chiefs fans let the football world know that Arrowhead was a tough place for an opponent to play. On national television they showed they were the best fans in the game.

We showed something, too, that night: when we were playing well, we could beat anybody in the sport. We did the same thing the following week when we went down to Miami and blew out the Dolphins 42–7. We'd thought we were the better team the year before when they'd beaten us in the playoffs and we'd circled that game on the schedule. And I rushed for 153 yards in that game—like I was picking up where I left off on that last drive before our season was cut down by that holding penalty that pushed us just out of Nick Lowery's field-goal range.

* * *

Any success I had that season and during my career wasn't just me; it was our offensive line as well, which was the best offensive line in the league. In 1991 those guys allowed the fewest sacks in the AFC and paved the way for my Pro Bowl season.

John Alt, our left tackle, had the perfect build for the position. A tall, former tight end who had the feet of a skill position player, Alt never talked. He was serious, and it seemed he never made mistakes on the field. Everything he did was precise. He made two Pro Bowls and is a member of the Chiefs Hall of Honor.

Our left guard, Dave Szott, was another guy who was serious about the game, which is why he played 14 years in the NFL and was named All-Pro in 1997. Szott is a guy with really good values. Long after our careers were over, I had a major operation on my spine in New Jersey, where Szott lives, and Szott came to visit me in the hospital. We hadn't been in contact in years, but he still made a point of dropping by. It was a very meaningful gesture. It showed that being a teammate means something beyond a business relationship. The great thing about sports is that it can forge those bonds.

At center was Tim Grunhard, another stalwart and member of the Chiefs Hall of Honor. Most of the linemen were quiet, but Grunhard was a talker. Centers are like the quarterbacks of the offensive line, and Grunhard was engaging, had a good sense of humor, and was a natural leader. He was one of the biggest centers in the league, and in short-yardage situations, I always knew that if I looked inside, I could make some forward progress there if I just followed Grunhard because he would always move the man across from him. Nowadays, Grunhard is a popular guy in the Kansas City area, where he does a lot of charity work with the Chiefs Ambassadors. He remains a good friend of mine.

Dave Lutz was our right guard. He played for a decade with the Kansas City Chiefs and was the definition of dependable. The continuity of our line was a big reason why it was so good. Lutz was a gentle giant type. The 6'6" Lutz liked to chew his tobacco, keep to himself, and focus on his work.

Rich Baldinger was our right tackle. Where most of our linemen were quiet and serious, Baldinger, who was undersized, drove himself with emotion. He was a talker—he's an analyst on TV like his brother, Brian—and he would get hyped during games and hype up other guys. Our line had a mix of personalities, and everybody clicked.

Jonathan Hayes was our tight end, but I can mention him when talking about our offensive line because he was such a great blocker. I give him a hard time. He's from the Pittsburgh area, but the guy thinks he's a cowboy. He talks really slowly like John Wayne. And after he retired from football, he bought a ranch outside of Kansas City with horses and everything. After that he got into coaching, becoming a well-respected tight ends coach. He was tight ends coach for the Cincinnati Bengals for 16 years, which is incredible and shows you the type of guy he is and how much people respect him. He remains one of my closest friends.

A running back absolutely needs to get along with their offensive linemen, and all of us certainly did. Every Monday we'd go out to dinner, usually to a restaurant owned by Lynn Dickey, the former Green Bay Packers quarterback who grew up in the area and played at Kansas State. We'd eat, have a few beers, and watch the *Monday Night Football* game. During my career I kept a low profile off the field and mostly kept to myself and my family, but those nights at that restaurant were some of the best memories I have.

But I can't talk about the offensive line without talking about a couple of guys who were gone by '91. The first is Irv Eatman, our right tackle my first few years. He coined my "Nigerian Nightmare" nickname and was extremely charismatic and personable, a great storyteller with a sharp wit. He was a freak athlete, an offensive lineman who didn't have an ounce of fat on him and could run like a skill position player.

And then there was Mike Webster, who was gone by '91, but whose impact was still being felt. When we got Webster from the Pittsburgh Steelers, he showed our team what being a professional was all about. Webster was 37 years old when he came to the Chiefs and had already established himself as a Hall of Famer, winning four Super Bowls with the Steelers and making nine Pro Bowls. For an offensive lineman, he was very small—he was noticeably smaller than I was—but he was extremely strong for his size and was the ultimate technician. He understood that football is a game of angles and leverage, and that preparation leads to success. He hardly talked, but he taught us so much.

He also taught the football world so many things after his retirement. The brain damage and CTE he sustained—and the homelessness and addiction that resulted—have all been documented. Anyone who saw the movie *Concussion* or has followed the conversation about CTE knows the story about how Webster's long, illustrious career actually ruined his life and led to his premature death at the age of 50. His brain was examined by Dr. Bennet Omalu. Like me, Omalu was a Nigerian immigrant who knew nothing about football when he came to America but learned that in this country football has a way of finding you.

When Webster was having his problems, I heard about what he was going through. It was just so sad because Webster had always used his smarts to put himself above the competition, but that very brain was causing him and his family all those problems. It made me sad and it also made me nervous. Everyone, who has ever played football for a long time, feels that way when they hear these stories—even if some deny it. It's human nature, and we all wonder: *Is the same thing gonna happen to me?*

*   *   *

In those days the AFC West was a premier division. In 1991 the division featured three playoff teams in us, the Los Angeles Raiders, and the Denver Broncos, who won the division. In those days half of your games were against the division, and there was less player movement than today, so all of those rivalries were even more intense because we'd go up against the same guys year after year.

Seattle was the toughest environment. I don't know if they called themselves the "12s" back then, but it was as loud then as it is now and maybe even louder because they played in a dome back then. I hated playing there. The turf was old, rock hard, and in tatters. It was in Seattle's Kingdome where I tripped over a fold and separated my shoulder back in '89. Another thing that made playing the Seahawks hard was that they had Dave Krieg, a steady, savvy quarterback who always seemed to kill us. (In 1992 we acquired him to be our quarterback.)

When we'd go to San Diego in December, I could feel the relief in my body because we were going to a warm climate and we were going to a grass field without having to deal with those crazy-ass Raiders fans. San Diego Chargers fans actually were nice. It was a laid-back, Southern California experience in every way except between the lines because I never had much success against the Chargers. They always had excellent inside linebackers. Gary Plummer was a really good player for years, and then in 1990, they drafted Junior Seau.

People always talked about the altitude in Denver, but it never impacted me. The fans were passionate and loud, but they really didn't compare to our fans. Denver Broncos fans are good fans. Kansas City Chiefs fans are *great* fans. John Elway, though, was a sight to behold. With his mobility and his incredible arm, he could make plays nobody thought possible. Watching him was different than watching other quarterbacks because at any moment he could throw a laser 60 yards downfield. When the play broke down, that's when Elway was at his most dangerous. I can still hear Marty Schottenheimer's voice, drilling it into our defense: "Keep him in the pocket!"

The Raiders always talked so much shit. They took after their owner. They talked like they were the baddest team in the league, but they weren't— it was easy to run on them. Their fans were the same way. They carried themselves around like they were intimidating, but they were just a bunch of clowns. During my career they played in the Los Angeles Memorial Coliseum, and that stadium never came close to selling out. It's hard to have the most intimidating atmosphere when your stadium has huge swaths of empty seats, but that's Raiders fans for you. The Coliesum was originally designed for the Olympics, so a track surrounded the field, and there was so much space between the field and the stands that it wasn't loud at all. The atmosphere wasn't intimidating, and neither were the Raiders' players.

And that leads me to Week 17 of the 1991 season. The Chiefs and the Raiders knew we'd play two straight games against each other: one to end the regular season and one in the playoffs. The winner of the Week 17 matchup would host the wild-card game between us the next week. Unfortunately, after a great year, I was breaking down by season's end with knee problems, so I played very little in Week 17. But Barry Word, who hadn't played as much in '91 as in his breakout '90 season, stepped right in and had a huge game, rushing for 152 yards and leading us to a 27–21 win. This gave us the home-field advantage the following week—which represented the Chiefs' first home playoff game since the 1971 season and the first playoff game in Arrowhead Stadium history.

I suited up, but at that point, I could hardly walk, so I got only one carry for two yards. But the atmosphere at Arrowhead was electric. This game was years—decades—in the making, and it came against our longtime, hated rival. It was an ugly, grind-it-out, 10–6 win, the best of Martyball. Even if it wasn't pretty, we found a way to get it done. And even though I didn't play a major role, I savored that win. As I've said before, I never really loved playing football. But what I did love was the camaraderie with my teammates and the connection with the fans. That day I felt like I was a part of the Arrowhead faithful in my adopted hometown of Kansas City, pulling hard for my guys.

The next week we went to Buffalo. I didn't play at all this time, and we got our asses kicked. The Bills completely flipped the script on us from that midseason game at Arrowhead, when I ran for two touchdowns and flexed my muscles in the endzone. In the playoff game, the Bills ganged up against the run and knocked Steve DeBerg out of the game with a thumb injury. They were fresh off their bye week, and the league still hadn't figured out their explosive, no-huddle offense. In 1991 they actually scored more points than they had the year before.

I remember sitting on the sideline, freezing my ass off in Buffalo. It had been a good season but didn't end as I'd imagined it, and I wondered how long I could keep playing. The Bills crowd was raucous, and the fans behind the bench were giving us a hard time. But as into the game as they were, I remember thinking, *This is nothing compared to Arrowhead.*

14

THE END OF THE LINE

Even though I could feel my body breaking down after the 1991 season, I wasn't ready to call it quits. If you're a veteran NFL player, you're never close to 100 percent anyway, and it's hard to tell just how wrecked your body is. Going into 1992, I felt I had more to accomplish as a player, and we had more to accomplish as a team.

There was also the financial component. I'm not ashamed to admit that a big reason I played was the money, and I wanted to keep playing to extend my earning years. By this point, I had my daughter Tiana to support. I'd also gotten very involved with charitable causes and I wanted to help as many people as I could. I had signed two contracts to that point, but before the '92 season, I signed my most lucrative deal, one which would pay me $1.17 million for that season and make me one of the league's highest-paid running backs. I had actually signed a deal for a lot less, but weeks later I'd seen a news report that Neal Anderson of the Chicago Bears was making $1.65 million, which was a lot more than I was. So I called Carl Peterson and said that if he truly felt that Anderson was more important to the Bears than I was to the Chiefs, we could keep the contract. But if he felt I was equally important or more so, I wanted a lot more money.

Peterson was known as a hard-ass negotiator, and for that reason, a lot of the guys didn't like him. But he was always loyal to me, and I thought he was a fair man. I think he respected that I took it upon myself to call him directly, so we tore up the contract from a few weeks prior and agreed to the deal that paid me $1.17 million for the '92 season.

I was always smart with my earnings. I put some money away in annuities and put most of the rest in the bank. My main goal when I turned pro had been to make my family more comfortable, so when I got my rookie contract, the first thing I did was move my dad and my remaining two siblings at home to a two-bedroom apartment in Enugu with a proper living room and kitchen, which is something I never had growing up. A few years later, I built from scratch an apartment complex in Enugu. My family lived in one of the units there and rented the other units out, and the rent money provided a steady source of income. The cost of developing land in Nigeria is about 10 percent of what it is in America, so my NFL money went pretty far. It was nothing extravagant, but it made their lives better. I'd always hear stories about professional athletes having to bankroll their entire families and I was very lucky my family wasn't like that. They never asked me for anything. They were proud people, and though I was happy to use my money to make them more comfortable, I never felt any pressure to provide for them.

My personal expenditures for the most part were also modest. Sure, I treated myself to things I wanted, but I don't have lavish tastes. For example, I bought a nice Mercedes four-door sedan but nothing crazy like four Lamborghinis. After my rookie year, I bought a four-bedroom house in Claremont, California, and signing that contract before the '92 season allowed me to pay off my mortgage. The house was one story and very practical; my one requirement was that I wanted enough space to have family members stay when they visited. Claremont is a nice college town about 10 minutes on the freeway from Azusa Pacific, where I worked out during the offseason and where I still considered myself part of the community.

Coach Franson and Coach Milhon and their families were still there. By that point my sister Obi, who went to Azusa for undergrad, was living in the area and so was my brother Emmanuel, who went to grad school there for business administration. Both stayed with me in my Claremont house when they first came to America, but they moved out after they got acclimated.

So going into '92, I had the big contract I'd always wanted. My goal was to play three more years and then retire. But my body had other plans.

*   *   *

My body finally said enough is enough in 1992. My shoulders, my knees, my back—which required three surgeries after my career—my head, even my fingers hurt.

I only started five games in '92. Mostly I was used in short-yardage and goal-line situations as a 31-year-old battering ram. I could still deliver a blow, but the cost of doing so kept getting higher and higher. All those collisions involved so much force, and even if I got the better of my opponents, I felt the impact in my shoulder, down my spine, and in my head.

I had never actually gotten over my shoulder injury I sustained in 1989 during that bull in the ring drill in training camp. Every time someone would hit me—whether it was in practice or a game—I felt something go down my arm. I shook it off, having no clue that sensation was nerve damage. With every hit the nerve damage, which has haunted me in the decades since, got worse.

In 1992 my numbers declined to 448 yards on 3.1 yards per carry. Everything was a struggle. I tried to block out the pain and focus on my job, which I was getting paid very well to do. But my mind wandered away from football. I'd never loved the sport itself and I couldn't help daydream about a life without this weekly punishment.

But the team continued to win. We had acquired Dave Krieg from the Seattle Seahawks to be our quarterback—Krieg had beaten us many times—and we went 10–6, making the playoffs as a wild-card. That was three straight trips to the playoffs and four straight winning seasons under Marty Schottenheimer. This was an amazing accomplishment, considering that in the 15 seasons before Schottenheimer and Peterson came to Kansas City, the Chiefs only had *two* winning seasons.

We were 9–6 going into our final game of the season at home against the Denver Broncos, where the winner would go to the playoffs and the loser would go home. It was a typical Arrowhead crowd, and we blew them out 42–20. Late in the game, I took a handoff and followed a good lead block by Kimble Anders—a Chiefs Hall of Honor member himself—and powered my way into the endzone, running over a couple of Broncos. It was a classic Christian Okoye run, the type I became famous for. It was our last score of the game—and as it turned out, it was the last points of our season and the last touchdown of my Chiefs career.

The following week, we went to San Diego to play the Chargers, who'd surprised everyone that year by winning our division on the strength of their great defense. I didn't play, and our team couldn't do much against that great defense, getting blanked 17–0 and gaining just 251 yards. That game exposed our shortcomings on offense; we'd finished 25th in the league in yards, which wasn't going to get it done for a team that thought of itself as a Super Bowl contender.

In response the organization changed its offensive philosophy. First, Schottenheimer brought in Paul Hackett, an expert in the West Coast Offense who'd been Joe Montana's quarterbacks coach with the San Francisco 49ers in the 1980s, as offensive coordinator. The next target was Montana himself, who had missed the previous two years due to injury but was now healthy and was available because Steve Young had established himself as a superstar. Wanting to play for a contending team, Montana chose the Chiefs over the Phoenix Cardinals. And suddenly, the Chiefs, who'd been trying to upgrade the quarterback position even long before I'd gotten there in 1987, had one of the best quarterbacks of all time.

This was all great for the Chiefs—Montana would lead them to the AFC Championship Game, where they again lost to the Buffalo Bills—but it meant the writing was on the wall for me. The West Coast Offense was basically the opposite style of the offense we'd run the previous few years. It was the opposite of Martyball, the system that Schottenheimer was putting in place when he called me in the spring of 1989 and told me, "Prepare yourself to run the ball."

My fate was sealed when the Chiefs signed Marcus Allen, a running back perfectly suited to the West Coast Offense because of his skills as a receiver. I was never much of a pass catcher ever since that day at Azusa Pacific when I picked up a football for the first time and said, "Very interesting but very impractical." After Schottenheimer became the head coach in Kansas City, I'd hardly ever been asked to catch the ball. My reception totals in those four years were two, four, three, and one, respectively.

These days, Allen is a friend of mine in Southern California. I always found it interesting that my career as a running back began when I saw Allen's beautiful run in the 1983 Super Bowl. If I was going to play football, I wanted to do that. And it ended—for all intents and purposes—when the Chiefs brought in Allen to replace me.

That year, 1993, I went to training camp, but during camp I injured my knee, which required arthroscopic surgery. The operation would've put me out for about a month, but Schottenheimer called me and said the organization planned to put me on injured reserve, meaning I'd miss several weeks. This seemed like confirmation that the Chiefs had moved on. I understood this and didn't feel bitter about it.

I told Schottenheimer that instead of going on IR I planned to retire. I still felt I could contribute and I still had a lot of money left on my contract. But there were just too many signs that it was time to go. My body had been giving me those signs for years. Schottenheimer tried to convince me otherwise, but I was firm in my convictions, and soon after the Chiefs and I came to an injury settlement, formally cutting ties with the team that drafted me. The only team I ever knew. The team I still love.

In the following months, I didn't miss the sport at all, but I did miss my teammates. I missed the locker room, I missed working out with the guys, I missed the joking around, I missed the sense of common purpose. The next spring the Los Angeles Rams got in touch with my agent and convinced me to come to their offseason practices. At that point I was feeling pretty adrift and alone, so I decided to give the Rams a shot.

But a handful of practices convinced me that my instincts a few months prior were correct: I didn't want to be a professional football player anymore. Practicing with another team felt weird. I wasn't remotely interested in learning a whole new offensive system. The drudgery of practice returned, and it reminded me how mentally difficult football is because of the mind-numbing repetition in addition to the physical pain. This time I was really done.

When I first came into the league, I had told myself I would play for three or four years. I wanted to see if I could succeed at the highest level. I wanted a little nest egg of money for my family and my future. I blew way past those goals and succeeded beyond my wildest dreams. I walked away from the game with no doubt I was making the right decision.

15

Depression

There were some other things going on that were making it hard to push through the pain on the football field. My baby Michael's death 23 minutes after being born in 1990 was the first thing. Then, in 1992 my dad died.

The trouble began in the months before the '91 football season, when my dad started having problems with his bladder and came to visit me in California. I was always trying to get him to move to the U.S., but he preferred to stay in Nigeria, which I understood. But one of the reasons I wanted him to come to America was the superior medical care, and in '91 when he was having those issues, I took him to get checked out. The doctors said his prostate was enlarged and they took him for a biopsy. His Prostate-Specific Antigen level was extremely high, but surprisingly no cancer was found.

Still, the doctors were very concerned. They said my dad needed to be monitored closely, and the office called me and sent me letters to schedule some follow-up appointments. But my dad didn't think he needed them. Because no cancer was found, he thought didn't need to worry about cancer. Convinced he had a clean bill of health, he went back to Nigeria. I tried to get him to come back, but he wouldn't listen. And then a year or so later, he started experiencing pain all over his body that very quickly became severe. The cancer that started in his prostate had spread to his bones.

I arranged for him to come back to the U.S. to get looked at, but by that point, it was too late. He was actually at my sister's place in Lagos, working out stuff for his visa, when he slipped and fell in her living room. His bones were so brittle that he broke his neck and back and became paralyzed. A week or so later, he died in the hospital. He was only 75 years old. Before the cancer he was in good shape physically. Mentally, he was just as sharp and smart as the guy I'd always known. Never once did I think of him as an old person, and his death is still a shock to me—something that's also true for my mom, who died at 55. Suddenly, there I was, a guy without parents, and it was disorienting. Even today I still can't really believe that my parents aren't living anymore.

It's just so sad: my parents struggled to provide for us all their lives. Then, because of football I had the ability to make their lives much more comfortable. But my mom missed out on that entirely, and my dad only got to experience any sort of comfort for just a few years.

My dad's death was a big blow. During this time my marriage was also crumbling. I met my wife Lauren at Azusa Pacific when I was a senior and she was a freshman. We dated my first three years in the league, doing the long-distance thing when I was in Kansas City and she was at school, and we got married in 1990. We hadn't lived with each other until we got married, but soon after we moved in together, it began to become clear we weren't a good match.

After Tiana's birth our differences really came to a head. Lauren's childhood had been traumatic, and her family had a lot of dysfunction. My childhood hadn't exactly been easy, but the solidness of my family's love was never in doubt. We were tight-knit and we looked out for each other, which wasn't the case with her family. Having a child brought out these differences in our outlooks.

One flashpoint was that during the season I wanted Lauren and Tiana to come to Kansas City as often as they could, but she preferred to stay in

California. This hurt me; it simply wasn't the way I'd envisioned married life and it was the clearest indication that we saw things very differently. I would always think back to my parents, who worked so well together and had very similar values. They were from the same hometown, they had the same loyalty to each other and their kids, and they both had the same vision for what a family should be. That wasn't the case with my marriage.

Soon, we began to argue about everything. And I mean *everything*—every silly little thing that I was shocked we disagreed about because I figured it would be so obvious. I'm not an argument guy; I'm a live-and-let-live guy. If you and I disagree, I'm not going force you or try to convince you of my side. But during the last couple years of my marriage, Lauren and I were arguing constantly; it was like my life at home was one never-ending argument. I hated arguing and yet I couldn't stop. It left me completely exhausted and frazzled.

I realize now it takes two to tango. We came from completely different upbringings and had different perspectives, and as I've gotten older, I've come around more to thinking that we were just incompatible—not that I was right and she was wrong. And in fairness I could have had a lot more patience at times. I also have to give her a lot of credit for the way Tiana turned out: we raised her with a 50/50 custody split, and Tiana turned into a remarkable woman, so Lauren must have been doing a lot of things right.

But we weren't right for each other and we finally separated in 1994. It was my decision. Lauren tried to salvage things, booking us a few appointments at couples' therapy. I went, but my heart wasn't into it. I knew the marriage wasn't right. So I just sat there bored, and what Lauren and the therapist talked about didn't seem to resemble the marriage I'd been experiencing. At a certain point it was over; we formally divorced in 1996 after the legalities were sorted out. I was tremendously relieved and I never regretted my decision. But for the first time in years, I was also alone—at least for the 50 percent of the time (per our custody agreement) that I didn't have my daughter. Being alone gave me the time to think about things I'd pushed to the back corners of my mind. That's when the depression set in.

*   *   *

I had never understood depression. I thought your happiness was something you could control. I grew up amid a brutal civil war, constantly moving homes to escape the shells overhead, and with the smell of death in the air. From an early age, I had developed the ability to roll with things and to see the best in people and situations. Everyone in my family is the same way: we've been through some hardships, but we always come through smiling. I'd hear about people who were depressed and, to be honest, I'd dismiss them: *Why can't they just think about things that made them happy?*

When I got hit with depression myself, I finally knew why they couldn't. I had been through a lot in a very short period: Michael's death, then my dad's death. In 1994 I officially retired from football, which, though I never regretted it, left a void and lack of purpose. I also had back surgery that year, which made it hard for me to move around. Even though I wasn't playing football anymore, my body didn't exactly bounce back good as new. The same went for the headaches that I'd always experienced, which never went away and are now worse than when I was playing. Then, there was the separation from my wife. That was straw that broke the camel's back.

For the next three years, I didn't do much of anything at all. I had my daughter half the time and was devoted to her, but after I dropped her off at school, I came home, worked out—even at the pit of my despair I never stopped working out—and then did nothing for the rest of the day. I'd sit in front of the TV and watch movies. I'd watch TV. I had no desire to leave the house or to do anything. I was unhappy at home but completely unmotivated to be doing anything different. I had no desire to see people.

I didn't watch the Kansas City Chiefs. It's not that I had bitter feelings; I just wasn't interested. I didn't miss football and I didn't miss my friends. I was just numb and bored, and everything felt heavy.

I kept it all to myself. I knew nothing about therapy—other than the couples therapy I'd gone to with Lauren, which did nothing for me. Because I didn't see any friends, nobody knew what I was going through, so all those feelings just festered inside me. When you're in a state like that, certain things cross your mind. I didn't seriously contemplate killing myself, but I did harbor the idle thought of suicide. It was one of many thoughts that came and went but didn't compel me to get off the couch.

During this time it never occurred to me that my depression might have been related to all the hits I'd taken and the headaches I was experiencing. I didn't think about the physiology of my brain. There were too many other factors to explain how I felt like having no job, no parents, and no wife. The idea of a happy family had gone up in smoke. But knowing what we know now, I think it's pretty obvious that the sport impacted me and I was struggling with moving on with my life with a damaged body and a damaged brain.

* * *

Finally, I pulled out of it. It was all because of my daughter. I didn't feel I had much to live for except for her, so I threw myself into being a girldad. I was lost in the world, but being Tiana's dad came naturally. I enjoyed every part of it—cooking for her, giving her baths, playing with her, walking with her to school. I taught myself to braid her hair. Seeing her grow up brought me pure joy. It lifted me out of the heaviness.

Tiana loved to sing—she still does. I'd play oldies music on the radio, and when she was a tiny girl, she'd sing along. She knew every word to Bob Marley's "Three Little Birds" from the time she could talk. Sometimes I'd put on a CD for her to start her on a song and then sit back and watch her as she sang and danced. It was a little performance for an audience of one. She actually reminded me of myself. When I was little, I'd do dances and perform for my siblings as well.

Now, Tiana's a 32-year-old successful actress, living in Hollywood about 45 minutes away from me, and I'm incredibly proud of her. She stars on the TV show *Panhandle*, but that came after years of hard work, when she was making fitness videos and taking lesser-profile acting jobs. I told her when she was a kid: "Don't wait for anybody to provide for you. Anything you want, you should be able to get for yourself." And she has taken that advice to heart. She knew what she wanted to be since she was little and went out and made it happen, which is another way she reminds me of myself. I saw that spark when she was a little girl. That spark brought me out of my stupor.

I have two other kids who are just as wonderful. My son, Kosi, is 19 and lives in Kansas City. I dated his mom, but it didn't work out, and now his mom and I don't get along. Kosi's a really good kid with a good heart, and I love him dearly, but I've never been able to spend as much time with him as I've wanted to. For years I wanted him to spend summers in California with me, but his mom didn't want that, and we fought about it in court, and I lost. The whole thing is painful for me. Kosi and I talk on the phone a lot, and I fly to Kansas City as often as I can to spend a couple of days, but it's obviously not the same as being with him for long stretches, and I feel like I was deprived of the opportunity to have the influence on him I wanted to have.

Kosi's a smart kid with an impressive emotional intelligence, where you can tell he's considering everyone's feelings. He's got a charming personality. When he was a kid, he would talk to everyone, and all my friends loved him. These days, like a lot of kids his age, Kosi is a bit lost and confused. I worry about him. As of this writing, he's not in college and he doesn't know what he wants to do with himself. He used to play basketball and baseball; when his mother and I fought in court about his summers, one of her arguments was that he should play sports in Kansas City with his friends. But now he doesn't like sports anymore. I've taken him to Kansas City Chiefs games, but he'll play video games on his phone, and it always pains me to see him retreat into that world. But I'm proud of him and I believe in him. He's a great kid. I'm here for him.

My youngest child, Laylah, is 17. The relationship between her mother and me didn't work out, but we get along well, which makes things a lot easier. Laylah lives in the Hesperia area, about 40 minutes away from me, and I see her all the time and talk to her every day.

Laylah is my athlete. She's an excellent volleyball player with aspirations of playing in college. Her personality is lovely. She's easygoing, respectful, and an excellent student. She's always smiling and laughing and is an absolute joy to be around. And she's fiercely determined. She recently suffered a serious knee injury, and the way she is rehabbing to return to the volleyball court makes me proud. She has the toughness and focus to succeed in sports and in life.

Her physical therapist is my good friend, Eddie Lange, who worked with me during my NFL career. He and his wife, Jessica, do a lot of work with me with my charitable foundation. During the holiday season, they started a tradition where we visit pediatric hospitals with a lot of our athlete friends.

As a father I always think back to my dad and the lessons he imparted in me. He spoke quietly but directly. If we did something wrong, he'd let us know, but if we did something right, he'd hug us and tell us as well. We always knew where we stood because he was completely honest and open with us. I strive to be the same kind of father to my kids. Being a father is the most important thing for me. It's what gives my life meaning. And it all started with Tiana, who injected meaning into my life when I was lost and depressed. She got me going, and then I started to live life again.

In about 1996, four years after I last played an NFL game, I finally was motivated to do something else with my life, so I opened a gym. Working out had always been my peaceful place. When I was depressed, my training gave me goals to set and meet, and before that, when I was constantly arguing with Lauren, I sought refuge in my machines and weights, which never argued with me. I operated that gym for a few years and I loved it. It gave me a chance to be around people and to feel their positive energy. I also opened a clothing store near Azusa Pacific, which didn't work out. But then I bought and ran a protein powder company, which I ran for about 14 years. I also stayed busy doing charity work and founded the California Sports Hall of Fame.

In 2000 I was inducted into the Chiefs Hall of Honor. It's an honor that means everything to me. Being among the great players and great men I met when I first came to the Chiefs makes me proud beyond words. That year I started going back to Chiefs games and catching up with guys I hadn't seen for a few years. Now going to Chiefs games is a regular part of my life. It took a while, but several years after my career ended, I was feeling like myself again emotionally. I was upbeat, motivated, happy with my lot in life.

But physically? Well, that was another story.

16

My Life of Pain

The state of my body—and the pain that I deal with in my daily life—are things I don't talk about with many people. People don't want to hear it. People prefer to imagine me with my big shoulder pads, leaning forward, as the defenders bounce off The Nigerian Nightmare. But that was a few fall Sundays a long time ago. Most of my life has been spent in the aftermath: three back surgeries, two knee surgeries, and a left knee that's currently bone on bone; a shoulder surgery and multiple separated shoulders that I learned to pop right back in, the pain always most excruciating right before the joint pops back into place and brings relief; and a torn bicep muscle that was never treated and now sticks out of my arm like a tennis ball.

Walking around is something I have to think about. For just the basic act of walking, I have to think about how to get going and about every step. Each step is careful. I'm always conscious of my back and knees. Any normal movement that you wouldn't think twice about is probably too abrupt for me. I may look imposing, but it's much easier to push me over than you.

If I've been sitting on an airplane for hours, after the plane lands, I can't just get up and walk down the aisle like everyone else. No way—if I did that I'd collapse in a heap. Instead, I slowly rise to my feet and then just stand there for about five minutes, feeling a tingling wash over my body. Sensation is returning—some of it but not all because every limb and extremity of mine is numb to one degree or another. The last place where sensation returns is my legs. Finally, I can transport myself but never quite normally and never without fear that my left knee will buckle and give out on me once and for all. I once ran a 4.33-second 40-yard dash at Azusa Pacific. Now I'm the slowest person getting off the plane by far—even slower than the folks who are a couple decades older than I am.

When I go down the stairs, I guarantee I'm slower than you. I cling to the banister, and much of my weight is on my arms. The feeling in my legs is spotty; they might stop working any moment. If I fall down the stairs, it's certainly possible I'll get paralyzed because my spine is in such disrepair.

I can't stand up for long periods of time. My legs always feel like I've just run 10 miles. I have balance issues; my gait isn't normal, and it often feels like I'm walking on a swaying ship. I most definitely can't run or even jog. If a dog ever started chasing me, I have no idea what I'd do. If I need to get something above my head—a wine glass on a high shelf, for instance—I take a moment to strategize about how to get it because at baseline my shoulders are in pain, and if I have to contort them in any way, the pain becomes excruciating.

I'm a side sleeper, but because of the condition of my spine and shoulders, I can only sleep on my right side. If I slept on my left side, my spinal cord would do things that would cause severe pain; my shoulder, in particular, would kill me. On the right side, there's still pain, but it's tolerable enough that sleep can overtake it for short stretches if I'm sufficiently exhausted.

During my career I was addicted to Indomethacin. I never thought about my habit as an addiction and as myself as an addict, but that's what it was. Now I take Aleve and recently I started supplementing that with CBD oil. It helps somewhat, but it doesn't take the pain away. Managing my pain is a constant preoccupation; in fact, you could say that it's my actual occupation. It's the first thing I think about when I wake up in the morning.

Not long ago, I was at a restaurant with a friend and was eating some soup and I noticed my hand was shaking. I made a note of it. Is it Parkinson's? I don't know. Maybe I don't want to know. It's like that with many things.

My body is in horrible shape and so is my brain.

I have headaches every day; often I need to sit in a dark room for hours with no light or stimuli at all. I've had tinnitus—a constant ringing sound in my ears—ever since my playing days, and in recent years, it has gotten a lot louder and more intrusive. Like my headaches, I don't know how bad the tinnitus is going to get in the coming years, and that scares me more than I can describe. We've all read about the former NFL players who die by suicide.

In 2010 or so, Dr. Daniel Amen in California was taking CAT scans of the brains of former NFL players and he took one of mine. Based on what he saw, Dr. Amen told me that in about 10 years I was going to start having cognitive problems. I'd seen enough guys have those problems that I knew they were hardly rare. When Dr. Amen told me that, it felt like a train was coming down the tracks, and there was nothing I could do to stop it.

I'm on medication for my memory loss; I see a doctor every three months to monitor my symptoms. It's not something that ever gets better, so it's about forestalling the inevitable decline as much as possible. Sometimes I'll go run an errand and I'll think to myself, *Did I shut my garage door?* I circle back to my house and about 40 percent of the time I've forgotten. I'm slipping much more than a 62 year old should be. It's frustrating but also scary because I wonder: *Where this is heading?* I have no idea, and it's not something I can control.

Another thing I can't control is my mood swings. My sister brought this up to me. She said I snap at her all the time, that I have a short temper in a way she's never seen before. Often I catch myself, and think, *Man, this is nothing; calm down.* I step outside myself and think, *This isn't me! I'm a patient, gentle, person—not this guy!*

But I played NFL football, so I know that in some way, my brain is not my own. I gave my brain to the game.

*   *   *

I always think back to that first stinger I sustained during the bull in the ring drill in training camp in 1989. That was my first spinal injury. I experienced temporary paralysis—15 or 20 seconds of it, which was certainly enough to make the fear of paralysis very real for me.

I got back to the field quickly, I led the league in rushing, I was AFC Offensive Player of the Year, I became a phenomenon, I made the first of my two Pro Bowls, and played three more years, succeeding beyond my wildest dreams. But then about a year after my career, I started feeling my index fingers go numb. A few weeks later, both hands were numb like I had two clubs at the end of my arms.

I figured the numbness stemmed from problems I was having with my back and I didn't think it was that big of a deal. I'd already had an operation in 1994 on my lower back, and it was as quick and easy as those things go and brought immediate relief. So, when I started having numbness, I went to a chiropractor for an adjustment, thinking it would solve the problem. It didn't. The next week I went back to the chiropractor for another adjustment. Before he adjusted me, he took an X-ray of my back and neck. He took one look at the X-ray and said he shouldn't have ever touched me. My back and spine were in bad, bad shape. I needed to go to a specialist.

Dr. Robert Watkins is the best in the business when it comes to the spine, but you never want to find yourself in his office. He took an MRI of me and then told me I had a serious case of spinal stenosis, a progressive narrowing of the spinal column. The problem was much worse than I could even imagine. My spinal column was closing up and squeezing the life out of my spinal cord, which was causing severe neurological issues. (By comparison an average office worker's spinal cord is basically insulated from ever being touched. Mine was being choked.)

Dr. Watkins told me the problem would only get worse and that my central nervous system would continue to deteriorate to the point of being non-functional. My only options were two major surgeries: a laminoplasty and a laminectomy—the latter a very serious operation that involved the insertion of titanium rods to stabilize my spinal column and open it up so that my spinal cord had room to breathe.

But there was a problem: both operations were extremely expensive. I can't remember how much exactly, but I think they were in the hundreds of thousands of dollars. I no longer had insurance through the NFL. (The fact that there's no health plan for retired players is a shameful thing, a moral disgrace.) At the time, just like I am today, I was buying my own insurance, but my spine problems were considered a preexisting condition so the surgeries wouldn't be covered. (This is a shameful aspect of the American health care system.) The upshot was that if I wanted to have the operation that Dr. Watkins said I desperately needed, I'd have to go deep into my retirement savings and cash out all my annuities. It was all devastating news and a cruel reversal of fortune. I worked my ass off for years and did everything the game of football asked of me. My reward for all of that was being faced with a choice: I could either go basically broke or I could live the rest of my life with a body that didn't work.

I chose the latter. I thought I could manage my neurological problems and, while I believed Watkins when he told me things would only get worse, I couldn't really fathom what that meant. That's probably just like how you, Dear Reader, can't truly fathom what it's like to live inside my body.

For the next decade and a half, I did my best to stay in shape and be healthy, but I was getting weaker. I still worked out, but by the late 2000s, I was lifting about half as much as I was before. The numb sensation I'd initially felt in my fingers and then my hands slowly came to encompass my entire body, including, most frighteningly, my stomach. It was a tingling, hot-and-cold sensation throughout my body. I remembered that exact sensation from the bull in the ring drill incident. It felt exactly like that the moment before I slowly regained feeling in my extremities—and the memory was eerie. In a way I'd never escaped that moment.

I was terrified. My body felt like it was dying on me one extremity, then one limb, and then one entire area after another. But I kept it all to myself. I didn't want to tell my family and get them worried, and it's not in my nature to discuss my problems publicly.

I obviously needed the laminectomy Dr. Watkins had recommended, but I couldn't figure out a way to pay for it. In this predicament I wasn't alone. During my career I'd gone to an event organized by Mike Ditka, who'd formed an organization raising money for retired NFL players who needed money for operations. He told stories about guy after guy who had to mortgage his home and his kids' college money to pay his medical bills.

I listened and admired what Ditka was doing and, of course, I felt sorry for those guys. It never occurred to me I'd ever be in that situation.

Fortunately, I eventually connected with a group in New Jersey who raised money for these operations for retired NFL players and worked with doctors to perform them. Initially, it was difficult to find a doctor to do my surgery. Most took one look at my spine and back and didn't want to touch me. They had the same reaction as my chiropractor friend when he saw my X-rays and thought: *One false move and this guy's paralyzed if not dead.* But in 2010 Dr. Arash Emami stepped up as the doctor brave enough to take the job on.

And it was a big job. Dr. Emami stabilized my spinal column by fusing eight vertebrae to two titanium rods, which were placed vertically for support. Sixteen screws were used, fusing every vertebra from C2 to T2, which stretch from my upper neck to the upper-middle portion of my back. Those screws and rods will remain there forever.

The recovery from surgery was incredibly painful, but it was a life-saving operation. Without that operation I would have no quality of life at all. The surgery essentially opened my spinal column and allowed my cord room to breathe, whereas before the column was pressed into the cord at various points. But Dr. Emami said this left me extremely vulnerable to catastrophic injury. "Christian, your situation is one where, if you had tripped and fell, you'd be paralyzed," Dr. Emami told me. "The smallest thing—being rear-ended on the road—would've paralyzed you."

I had no idea how bad things had gotten. After that I began to recover some strength back but not even close to all of it. My right calf is numb; my thighs have some numbness and so do my arms. My central nervous system is damaged. My body simply doesn't work properly. The Nigerian

Nightmare, the baddest dude on the field from your memories, is far less physically capable than the average 62-year-old man.

And that tingle. It's not as pronounced as it was, but it's still there and it's unignorable. I'm not that old and I want to live a long time. But every movement reminds me of those few years back in my 20s and 30s when I took a chance on this peculiar American game. I remember being at Azusa Pacific for my first training camp when my body hurt all over, and I thought, *This isn't a game—this is crazy!* Now, every second of every day and every night, my body tells me I was right.

*   *   *

More than a decade ago, I joined the class-action lawsuit by former players against the NFL—the so-called "concussion lawsuit." It's obvious that what the NFL did was wrong. They knew the brain damage the sport inflicted, they knew that us players didn't, and they went to great lengths to keep us in the dark. Everyone, who has read anything on this topic, knows the deal. We have my fellow Nigerian, Dr. Bennet Omalu, to thank. (Dr. Omalu is an Igbo as well.)

The plaintiffs eventually came to a settlement with the NFL in 2013. The way they determined how much money, if any, each player would get was to put guys through a series of tests to show cognitive decline due to brain trauma. But when guys started getting settlements, it seemed to me that a lot of Black players that deserved big settlements weren't getting them. What was going on?

In 2021 we found out the NFL was engaging in race-norming. The practice assumes Black players start off with inferior cognitive function. This makes it harder for Black players to show cognitive decline, which reduces the settlement monies being paid out. Yes, you read all that correctly. This isn't a conspiracy theory; the NFL admitted to this, and it was a story for a day or two before the media moved on. But I didn't move on. As a Black person, it's incredibly disrespectful and hurtful. It's dehumanizing. It shows that the oldest form of American racism—the assumption that Black people are inferior—is alive and well in the present day. Whoever says racism in America is a thing of the past should think about this.

In my case, the way I was treated after the settlement was even more disrespectful—if that's even possible. After I took my initial test, I was never notified what my score was. I called and called and never heard anything back; it was confusing and frustrating. A bit later I received an email telling me I hadn't been given a score. I contacted a lawyer and after some digging I learned why. The NFL assumed I didn't understand the questions or the content of the test because I was from Africa, and they assumed I didn't speak English. They threw away my test and didn't think twice about it. In the minds of the NFL, I was worse than Black—I was from Africa, so my presumed intellectual deficits were off the charts.

I've never felt more insulted in my life. I'm a guy who graduated from college. All my siblings are educated. My father was an educator. My home country values education as much as any place on earth, which is why Nigerian Americans are among the most educated, successful demographics. The NFL basically told me that because of where I came from and the color of my skin that none of that meant anything.

When I learned about what they'd done to me, I thought back to how eager the NFL was to market me during my career: the nickname, The Nigerian Nightmare, and the whole backstory they peddled, as if the great American game delivered me from a life of hardship and starvation in the

African bush. In 1990, as part of a promotion for a preseason game in Berlin, Germany, we played against the Los Angeles Rams, they photographed me and Rams quarterback Jim Everett at the Berlin Wall. We had chisels and we took down tiny pieces of the wall. The message was clear: I have fame, riches, and success thanks to football and America. Football is America, and America is football.

Three decades later, I agree—only I'm seeing a different side of that. Since America's founding, the ugliest forms of racism and greed have been intertwined. That was true in 1619 when they first started bringing over African people. It's still true today. I think very highly of Lamar Hunt, so I don't believe this is true of all individual owners, but collectively the NFL owners have a slave masters' mentality.

After the race-norming became public, the NFL walked back the policy, and now they're going back and having Black players retake the tests. The NFL or any corporate entity only does the right thing when they're forced to, and this was no different. During the process of writing this book, I was finally allowed to retake the test. I'm happy about that, I guess, but I'll always feel betrayed and I'll always have a bitter taste about the sport.

Given the NFL's corporate practices and given my injuries, I'm very conflicted about my football career; there's no easy way to resolve it. I never loved the game of football, but I did love aspects of it—the camaraderie, the setting and achieving of goals, the connection to the fans and the community. Yet there is so much that's terrible about football and the NFL, so there's no neat way to encapsulate all those feelings.

Football brought me to America and provided a better life for me and everyone around me, including my children. That means a lot, and if I had to do it all over again, I'd do it again for that reason. But I don't know what's in store for me. We've all seen the many NFL lives that end in tragedy, even though most of these sad stories are kept out of the public view. In 10 years will I still say I don't regret playing football? I honestly don't know.

*   *   *

A few years ago, I had prostate cancer. Like more than 18 million Americans, I'm a cancer survivor. I'd always been diligent about getting my prostate exam because prostate cancer killed my father, ravaging his body in a year's time. My ordeal began when my PSA (Prostate-Specific Antigen) count leapt from 2.7 in 2019 to 4.7 the next year. A subsequent biopsy showed cancer in a prostate nodule.

Hearing the news from the doctor stopped me cold. *Cancer. Death.* You don't know what it's like to wrestle with these things until they're actually on the table.

I worried for my life, of course, but then I worried about telling people and how they'd react. How would I tell my loved ones? I had no idea and I felt frozen in time like I couldn't move forward. I didn't want pity from them and I didn't want to see them worry because that would make me worry even more.

Telling my children was the hardest. It took me a long time to tell Tiana. It took me even longer to tell my younger children, Kosi and Laylah. How do you communicate something like that to your kids? To me it seemed like there was no good answer, so I put it off as long as possible.

As for treatment I weighed my options. One friend had gotten radiation. Surgery to remove the prostate was another option, and though I worried how that would impact my sex life, a doctor reassured me things would be okay in that department. I thought about it for a bit. Sleep was even harder to come by than usual during that period. My mind went everywhere, and I thought about my kids a lot. *Am I gonna see my kids grow up? Am I gonna walk my daughters down the aisle when they get married? What's it gonna be like for them to not have their father there?*

I sought solace in God and prayed every night. I prayed that God would give me the wisdom to make the right decision. And God answered my prayers. I chose the surgery to remove the prostate. The surgery was November 2, 2020, and I've been cancer-free ever since.

After the surgery, though, I had a terrible experience in the hospital. The pain was much worse than I could've possibly imagined, like a flaming stick was being shoved into me. My main nurse completely lacked empathy. I'm not one to complain about the service, but that woman shouldn't be in that profession. I didn't know it at the time, but a few days later after I got home, I noticed some swelling in my lower stomach area where my catheter had been. My doctor told me I was probably having an allergic reaction to latex.

Tiana picked me up from San Antonio Regional Hospital in Upland, California. What an angel! There was an arrangement of flowers on the table, and she'd taken the entire week off work to look after me. The next few days were awful, but I got calls from so many people in my life, stretching back years. When you're in that situation, when the word "cancer" hangs in the air, you realize how precious life is. You realize nothing is more important than your people. For all you men out there: get your PSA screenings. Don't mess around with that. It could very well mean the difference between life and death.

17

NFL COMMISSIONER OKOYE

I believe the NFL is a players' league. The fans aren't paying to watch the owners, the referees, or the coaches. They're paying to watch the players perform amazing physical feats on every play. I also believe the only people who truly understand what it's like to be an NFL player are the players themselves. For that reason I believe a former player should run the league. Putting a player in charge would be best for the long-term health of the players and the sport itself.

I've often fantasized about what I'd do if I were commissioner. Sure, it's an idle fantasy—that day isn't coming anytime soon, and I'm not sure I'd even want that job anyway. But I have some ideas for how the league should be run:

1. Health insurance for all players for life

The league is built on the physical sacrifices of players; the injuries we suffer last a lifetime. Meanwhile, there's plenty of money to make this happen, and it's the right thing to do. The way things stand now, there are too many stories of guys choosing between spending their savings or getting the medical care they need; I was in that situation myself. That simply shouldn't be.

It's all part of the every-man-for-himself culture of America. For some reason Americans fear universal health insurance; they've been brainwashed by scare words like "socialism," even though most people have no idea what that means. Most Americans don't realize they have universal health insurance in places like the United Kingdom and Canada, and those countries are doing just fine.

Retired players get forgotten about because their interests are left out of the collective bargaining agreements negotiated between the owners and the players' union, which looks out for the interests of active players at the expense of the retired ones. My good friend Eric Dickerson has been very critical of DeMaurice Smith for being shortsighted, and I'm 100 percent with Dickerson. We need the NFLPA to fight, but it seems like Smith never does, selling out the players' long-term well-being for the sake of keeping the peace.

This all came to a head on January 2, 2023, in Cincinnati, when Damar Hamlin's heart stopped on the field. It looked at first like the nightmare scenario we all know is coming one day: the death of a player on an NFL field. If not for the heroism of the first responders, Hamlin—who we've learned is a great, compassionate human being—would not be alive. While Hamlin was getting CPR that saved his life, we now know that the NFL was planning to finish the game. It was the Buffalo Bills' and Cincinnati Bengals' players and coaches who stepped in and said they couldn't play. The NFL quickly backtracked and denied this, which they always do. Within a day or two, every team had changed their social media profile photos to Hamlin's jersey and lit a No. 3 on their stadiums in his honor. And when Hamlin recovered, the league spun it as one big, heartwarming story. It was another triumph over adversity brought to you by the NFL! And then everyone moved on. The playoffs were coming after all.

But you know who didn't move on? Those of us who have played this game and know its dangers—and know how little the league cares. A few days after Hamlin collapsed, there was a clip circulating on social media of Garrett Bush, a sports talk show personality in Cleveland, pointing out all the ways the NFL leadership were a bunch of hypocrites. The clip went viral on social media and it went viral among former players. This man's words rang true with so many of us. Bush, a former college football player, pointed out that if Hamlin never plays another down in the NFL, he wouldn't get another dime. His salary isn't guaranteed, and he hadn't been in the league long enough to get vested into the pension system. (Afterward, the Bills guaranteed his contract through the 2022 season. It's possible the Bills and the league will take care of Hamlin—for public relations reasons, no doubt—but nobody will take care of the many guys just like him who suffer a debilitating injury early in their careers that leaves them with medical bills for life.)

Bush also noted that when it comes to reviewing disability claims, the NFL has a private board with the league's own doctors who can override the assessments of the social security administration. You might be deemed disabled by the U.S. government, but your claims can be denied if the NFL's doctors don't agree. Another thing Bush noted: in the last CBA, the maximum disability payout dropped from $22,000 a month to $4,000 a month. This is a very, very big deal to many people, but most fans are unaware it happened because it was probably buried at the bottom of some article if it was reported on at all. The NFL's public relations machine is extremely effective.

Bush also pointed out that since the CTE settlement was reached in 2013, the league has paid out only 6.5 percent of the allocated dollars. There are so many guys who need this money now. I know many of them personally; they are suffering and so are their families. But the league doesn't care. If I were commissioner of the NFL, the league would care.

2. Mandatory retirement after 10 years in the league

This would accomplish two things. First, it would open up spots for more players. Millions of American kids dream of playing high-level professional football, but with the collapse of leagues like the USFL, though it's back on a smaller scale now, and NFL Europe, fewer guys have that opportunity. Second, it would cut down the health risks longtime players subject themselves to. I look at my friend Mike Webster, who played 17 years in the league, but his post-career life was tragic. Would Webster's story have been different if he'd gotten out after 10 years? Maybe. Not all NFL players make big money—many of the guys who fill out a 53-man roster do not—but 10-year veterans get paid a ton of money these days, so they won't be deprived.

3. More Black people in leadership positions

This isn't news to anybody: Approximately 60 percent of the league's players are Black, but there are no Black owners, and Black executives and head coaches are few and far between. We need to take proactive measures to change this, starting with recruiting potential Black owners. We also need a much bigger investment in helping players transition from the field to front-office positions. This would begin to build a professional network of Black people in the NFL, which is the only way to begin to redress a situation the league should be embarrassed about.

4. Require teams to do much more to give back to their home cities

Taxpayers in cities these days foot the bill for state-of-the-art stadiums, which allow billionaire owners to line their pockets. Ticket prices continue to rise, pricing the average fan out of going to a game. Increasingly, going to an NFL game is something only wealthy people can afford; there are families who save up all year to go to one game, sacrificing a vacation. The NFL can—and should—do better.

There are so many good people employed by the NFL; countless players and coaches volunteer their time and money in inner-city schools, hospitals, and other places where they're needed. Is it too much to ask franchises to make a commitment like the individuals they employ do? If I were commissioner, each team would have to sponsor inner-city schools in their home communities, makings sure they have computer labs, gym equipment, and properly-working facilities. There's so much need out there, and the NFL has so many resources at its disposal. NFL franchises are arguably the most beloved corporations in America—just think about the low-income kids spending hundreds of dollars on jerseys and other merchandise—and it's long overdue for these teams to return the love. Want to get kids off the streets? How about a beautiful new gym with basketball courts, a weight room, and a swimming pool with the team's logo on it? Are you telling me that won't attract all those kids out there in the quarterback's jersey? NFL teams get the benefits of being civic institutions. They should make good on the obligations of having this status.

From what I've seen, the Kansas City Chiefs do more than any other team when it comes to helping charities in their home city. The Chiefs Ambassadors, which I'm a part of along with many other former players, are extremely active, and the Chiefs support our work. The Chiefs are a good model; the league on the whole needs to do much more.

5. Investing more in expanding the game overseas and in Africa in particular

My success in the NFL made American football popular back home. Now, the NFL is filled with Nigerian American players, and I played a big part in that. In an ESPN.com article about my impact, former Chicago Bears Pro Bowl defensive end Adewale Ogunleye called me "the Godfather" and said my achievements were "like folklore" to Nigerians. Former Green Bay Packers running back Samkon Gado, who led the team in rushing in 2005, said he wore No. 35 because of me. When I was having success with the Chiefs, people in Nigeria started watching football, and the seed was planted. I always think back to when I came to the U.S. and watched Hakeem Olajuwon star at the University of Houston, which was the first time I'd watched basketball.

Spearheaded by Osi Umenyiora, the former star New York Giants defensive end who spent much of his childhood in Nigeria before coming to America, the NFL has taken some steps to expand into Africa. Umenyiora, who works for the league, is doing a great job, but the league needs to make a bigger commitment. I've been trying for several years to have the NFL hold a game in Nigeria, but the league has turned me down. One of the influential decision-makers told me confidentially that there's just not enough money in it for the NFL, which is disappointing to hear and, in my opinion, very shortsighted.

Under Commissioner Okoye, the game would expand to Africa and other places. It's hard for people who have lived their whole lives in America to realize this, but there's a whole world out there.

18

My Reality TV Career

I did the reality TV thing in the 2000s, when that stuff was becoming popular. I'd been out of the league for a little more than a decade, and while my body was already breaking down pretty badly, it looked good on TV. The first show I did was *Pros vs. Joes* on Spike TV. I received $25,000. I was curious, and it seemed fun. Plus, I'm always someone who embraces challenges.

I met up with a guy who runs a boxing gym and trained for about a month. One of the first things I learned was that even just keeping your hands up for an entire round is exhausting. I had a lot to learn; I'd maybe been in two fights in my entire life, and both occurred when I was a kid. I'd never punched anyone in the face.

My opponent was James Wilder, the former star Tampa Bay Buccaneers running back, and the fight was in Tampa. Wilder was much more refined than I was; he knew what he was doing, and I didn't. When I got into the ring, it was scary: there was a guy across from me who was trying to knock me out. It reminded me of my first days on the football field at Azusa Pacific, when I realized the guys on defense were trying to hurt me. Just as I did then, I wondered what I'd gotten myself into.

Immediately, my training went out the window, and I just started swinging on James. I didn't really connect with anything, but Wilder landed *his* punches to my chest, shoulders, forehead. It hurt a lot, but I managed to

202 THE NIGERIAN NIGHTMARE

go three rounds with him. The judges ruled it a split decision. They got that one wrong. Wilder was definitely the better fighter. Maybe they thought I was landing more of those punches than I actually was.

My next fight was in Caesars Palace, against former New York Giants linebacker Gary Reasons. The morning of the fight, Reasons called me in my hotel room. He told me his wife was terrified I was gonna kill him and basically said, "Let's just fake it the first two rounds; we'll fight in the third."

That sounded good to me. So that's what Reasons and I did. Unfortunately, the crowd wanted more action, and they started booing us. In the third round, Reasons came out and threw his first hard punch, getting me in the chest, and it hurt. I said to myself, *Okay, it's on now.*

Reasons went to throw another punch, but before he did, I caught him with a right to the side of the head. I hit him in just the right spot and I knocked him out. That was it for me. My boxing career ended with a record of 1–0–1.

I did another reality show in 2007 just for the heck of it. It was called *Pirate Master* and it was one of those shows by *Survivor* creator Mark Burnett. The premise was that we were all together on a boat—a pirate ship—off the Caribbean island of Dominica. We had to do various treasure hunts on the shore, after which the weakest link got voted off. I had no idea what I was signing up for and I regretted the whole thing immediately. We spent days on this ship, and I was miserable the entire time. The show wound up getting canceled before the season finished airing. It was a disaster all around.

One of the planned treasure hunts involved swimming from our boat to the shore and then finding the buried treasure, but the shore was about 400 yards away. When they told us the plan, I wasn't having it. "I'm not gonna do that," I said.

I'm not a swimmer; I know how to swim, but I'm not very efficient. When I was a kid, we'd go to my grandparents' place in Agukwu Nri in the countryside. There was a lake nearby, and my grandfather was terrified us kids would drown in it. So, when I was about 12, he called over one of my uncles and said: "Teach these kids how to swim!"

My uncle took me into the water, where there was a steep drop-off where the lake went from shallow to deep. We walked out there in the water, and then he picked me up and threw me into the deep part. "Swim back to the shore," he said.

It was about 15 yards away, and I panicked and flailed but somehow got back. That was all the swimming instruction I'd had. So when the *Pirate Master* people asked me to swim 400 yards after I'd been seasick for a week…well that just wasn't going to happen. After I spoke up, a couple of other people did, too. So they brought the boat closer to shore until it was about 100 yards offshore. I swam, but even doing that was exhausting and terrifying.

I wound up getting voted off the show early; I was the second person to leave. When they kicked me off, I knew the producers would want me to act like I was mad, so that's what I did. But I actually was ecstatic. I went back to the lodges where we stayed on this beautiful tropical island and, for the next few weeks until the filming of the show was over, I drank multiple pina coladas every day and ate delicious food. Everything was fresh—coconuts for the pina coladas, plantains, goat, and also fish right out of the ocean. I gained 45 pounds and was in heaven. And that was the end of my reality TV career.

19

GIVING BACK

So many people have helped me out along the way, and without those people, you wouldn't have heard of me and wouldn't be reading this book. In other words, one person's success isn't ever completely their own. We're all in this together, and just as people helped me, it's now my responsibility to help those who come after me.

For the past couple of decades, most of my day-to-day life has been dedicated to charity work. I made a lot of money when I was young and I was smart about saving it and investing it and now I get to focus on work I'm passionate about. I'm actually more passionate about charity work than I was about football, the thing that put me in position to do this in the first place. I launched the Christian Okoye Foundation in 1990 with a mission to help underprivileged and at-risk kids while using sports as a vehicle to help them stay on the right track academically. I know from experience that sports is the only thing that keeps many kids engaged. I was one of those kids myself.

The foundation, which I started during my playing career, impacts about 500 kids per year mostly in the Southern California and Kansas City areas. I use my connections with other professional athletes to run sports clinics in the inner cities; we partner with the Ontario-Montclair School District in California to run clinics. Most of the athletes who help me with the foundation grew up poor like I did, and our message to these kids is powerful: if you focus and set goals, you can achieve great things in this world. We also make regular visits to pediatric hospitals and, each holiday season in Kansas City, we take more than 200 kids shopping for gifts. In short, we show these kids that they matter. I've been doing this for more than 30 years and I've seen a lot of these kids grow into adults with families and good careers. There's nothing more rewarding that seeing that.

In 2006 I launched the California Sports Hall of Fame, a nonprofit organization that honors the many athletic heroes in California sports history and also puts on sports clinics for low-income kids. The list of inductees in the Hall of Fame features some of the best athletes of all time: Magic Johnson, Billie Jean King, Willie Mays, Joe Montana. It's a great way to connect the sports world to the many underprivileged kids in the area.

I do most of the work for the foundation and Hall of Fame myself. It's rewarding, but it's also overwhelming. If you're not spending your time doing this kind of work, it's easy to miss how much suffering there is in this world and in this country. In a place like the United States, the richest country in the world with its many billionaires, this simply shouldn't be. That there's so much wealth, yet so much need, reflects a society that doesn't have its priorities in the right place.

In recent years I've expanded the focus of my charitable endeavors to include Africa. Nine years ago I started running a soccer clinic in Enugu that meets once a week. I have top level soccer coaches, and the goal is the same as my foundation in the United States: use sports as a vehicle to give kids a sense of purpose and let them know they're important.

My current goal is to build a school in Nigeria. As of this writing, I had purchased a large property in Enugu and planned to start construction in the coming months. My hope is to have it open by 2024. The school will focus on trades like car repair, plumbing, and even computer technology. It will be aimed at the poorest kids for whom college might not be a possibility. These are the kids who need help the most; I want to show them that they still have a place in the world's economy. They're capable of having a good life, and my school will point them in that direction. My school, of course, will also emphasize sports. I plan to build a football field, hope to start a flag football program, and plan to lean on the NFL to lend a hand. The poorest places in the world are filled with talented, driven kids who just need an opportunity, and I'm doing my part to give them one. It's the right thing to do. People in my life did that for me.

*   *   *

I believe that athletes are role models. We've become famous and rich because of the adulation of the public. Therefore, we have an obligation to be people of whom the public can be proud. Many guys I played with have been great role models. The Chiefs Ambassadors and all the great work we do in the Kansas City community come to mind.

Athletes and other famous people are always in the spotlight, and everything we do has ripple effects. I was reminded of this a few years ago at a charity event hosted by my friend and former Kansas City Chiefs player Deron Cherry, which many former players attended. I went to the event and had a good time, but a few months later, Cherry came up to me and said, "Hey, Christian, is everything okay with you? You doing okay?"

I had no idea what he was talking about, but I said, "Yeah, of course." And I asked "Why?"

He explained to me why he was concerned. Apparently at his event, there was someone going around having all the ex-players sign two footballs. The person approached someone thinking it was me, but that person didn't sign his name. Rather, on one ball he wrote "Santa," and on the other ball he wrote "Huge Johnson." It was a stupid, vulgar joke—not at all funny and rude to the person getting the football signed. For me, it meant that many people were under the impression that *I* had written those things.

That really pissed me off at the time; it still does because it dragged my name through the mud. For all I know, there are people out there who still think I wrote those vulgar things. The incident shows that as athletes, even as former athletes, people are paying attention to what we do. Everything we do matters.

Unfortunately, since Donald Trump's rise, it seems like being a good person has become optional for American public figures. Telling the truth, believing in facts, showing basic respect and decency, you no longer have to inconvenience yourself by doing any of that—especially if you're a politician appealing to Trump's base.

Let me be perfectly clear: Trump is the exact opposite of everything that I aspire to be. The fact that people think he's some big, macho man is baffling to me because it's so obvious that he's basically a 10 year old with emotional problems in a grown man's body. He used his father's wealth to dodge military service, concocting an absurd excuse about bone spurs in his heel, and he goes around acting like some tough guy? Please.

It blows my mind that *this guy* turned our democracy upside down. *This guy* is the cult leader whose followers who would do anything for him, even die for him, which is exactly what happened with the hundreds of thousands of people who followed him into believing that COVID-19 wasn't real and died as a result. Most of what comes out of Trump's mouth are lies, but the truest thing he ever said was that he could walk down Fifth Avenue and shoot someone, and his supporters wouldn't abandon him. He was absolutely right about that, and this is more disturbing than most people can really grasp. Historians will look back on this time and wonder how someone, who told us he admired dictators and wouldn't respect the democratic process, got elected anyway.

His lying, his cynicism, and his disrespect for our country's core values have corrupted the entire world. I'm not exaggerating when I say this: America exports all aspects of its culture and politics, and throughout the world since Trump, we're seeing demagogues who bully and lie their way to power. Before Trump you couldn't just deny facts. You couldn't act like science didn't exist. You couldn't just claim you won an election that you had lost.

To watch American democracy attacked by America's very own president was shattering to me because I grew up thinking of America as a beacon of democracy. I was aware of America's many flaws. If you grow up in Africa, you're familiar with the horrors of colonialism, and I never thought America was perfect. But democracy itself seemed sacred. Then along came Trump, and the whole world learned how fragile it all was. Now, the genie is out of the bottle.

The same goes for xenophobia and racism. It's downright terrifying what so many people in this country think, which is something I see now on a daily basis on social media. I come from Africa—from one of the countries Trump might refer to as a "shithole," even though Nigerians are among the most educated, high-achieving immigrant groups in the world. I am a Black man—and yet the president of my country has linked arms with the most racist elements of society, which is why you see all those Confederate flags at Trump rallies. I thought I knew what this country was about. It turns out I had some things to learn.

Throughout my life, I've prided myself on my ability to get along with all kinds of people. My experience as an American has been overwhelmingly positive—no question about it. (I've lived two-thirds of my life here.) But the past several years have left me with a bitter taste. The hate that Trump unleashed has shown people's true colors, revealing what many people have been thinking all along but were too afraid to say. In the last several years, I've lost more than a handful of friends—or "friends," I should say. If I wasn't an athlete, what would these people think of me?

The COVID-19 pandemic was extremely upsetting. Getting through it without a catastrophic death toll required listening to experts and making the smallest sacrifice: wearing a mask in public places when the virus was raging during the pandemic's early stages. But too many Americans didn't care about all those people dying. They cared more about their supposed "rights"—to not wear a mask, to not take a safe vaccine—than they did about all that suffering. It was so immature with such deadly consequences. It took me back to when I first encountered Americans in Europe, when I was a teenage discus thrower competing in tournaments. The Americans would make too much noise in restaurants or disrespect the local customs, but when they were called out on it, they would always assert their "rights." They didn't seem to understand that as human beings we live in a society, and that individual rights have limits because everything is collective.

It also bothers me that America and other Western countries aren't more proactive against corrupt foreign rulers. In fact, as we know from colonialism and the Cold War, America has propped up many terrible heads of state. That's not right, and if this country truly sees itself as a moral example for the world, it should place serious sanctions against rulers who steal from their people to enrich themselves. If the international community led by the U.S. doesn't do that, many third-world countries don't stand a chance. This creates the kind of global inequality that leads to the flood of immigrants wanting to get into the U.S. and other Western countries, which so many Americans have such a problem with. Immigration is a huge sore point in politics these days, and right-wing leaders are rising to power on anti-immigrant platforms. But if we want to reduce immigration, we have to reduce the demand for it. The best way to do that is to make third-world countries more livable.

America also needs to get serious about getting guns off the streets. The rates of gun violence in this country are absolutely staggering compared to other Western countries. The firearm homicide rate in America is 22 times higher than those in the European Union. This is absolutely crazy. The regular mass shootings, including those in elementary schools in which little kids are murdered, are unique to America. It was shocking to me that the Sandy Hook shooting didn't lead to sensible gun reform. By the time of the Uvalde shooting nearly 10 years later, the lack of meaningful action was predictable. It boggles my mind that American police forces don't support stricter gun control, but with the political alignment the way it is, cops tend to side with Republicans, who have been bought off by the gun lobby. This is a terrible state of affairs, a tragedy that plays out every single day in dead bodies and grieving parents. America must do so much better.

All of that said, I'm an optimist by nature. When you grow up like I did, not knowing when my next meal would be and if the roof over my head would be bombed out, you develop these adaptive mechanisms. And despite all the ugliness that has been revealed the last few years, I remain optimistic. I look at it this way: Trump ultimately failed—he lost reelection in 2020 and his acolytes did terribly in the 2022 midterms—and the many imitators he spawned will also fail. Despite what we've seen in the past few years, America is a fundamentally good place, and good will prevail. I have faith in God that it will happen. I have faith in my adopted country that it will happen. I've been in America for more than 40 years. I've met too many good people to believe otherwise.

*　*　*

I owe my NFL career to so many people. And there are so many people who have made my journey so enriching. David Cross was a bartender at Kelly's, the beloved bar in the Westport neighborhood of Kansas City. Kelly's is a Kansas City institution and so is Cross, who started bartending after graduating from the University of Kansas in the 1980s and has been there for all the decades since. He used to have red hair, so everyone calls him "Red Cross," though by now his hair is all white. Red Cross was a classic bartender who could talk to anybody about any topic—and I mean *deep* conversations. He's beloved by all the Chiefs players throughout the years, myself included, and he's a connecting hub for the whole city. It seems like everybody knows him. Whenever I'm in Kansas City, I make it a point to go to Kelly's to see Red Cross.

Someone else who seems to know everyone in Kansas City is Tammy Neros, who works at the Westin at Crown Center and is a close friend to generations of Chiefs players. Neros is a wonderful lady who does a lot of work with the Chiefs Ambassadors, helping me and many of my fellow ambassadors hold charity events. She's a problem solver. If you need something, Neros gets on the phone, makes one phone call, and you're all set. Every time I go to Kansas City, I call her, and she books me a room at the Westin. The same is true for countless Chiefs players for decades.

I'm in touch with all my friends from the sports journey who brought me to America, starting with Innocent Egbunike, who still lives in Southern California more than 40 years after blazing the trail for all of us Nigerians to come to Azusa Pacific University. Without Egbunike you wouldn't have heard of me. Egbunike and I don't see each other that often, but our bond is unbreakable. He was the first bridge from Nigeria to America. I owe everything to him.

I'm in touch with other track guys from those teams. I stayed close with Blackman Ihem until his 2021 passing. I'm still close with Cres Gonzalez, who still knows how to speak Igbo purely from hanging out with a group of Nigerian guys all those years ago in college.

I'm still very close with Coach Milhon and Coach Franson. I sometimes have dinner at their houses, just like I did in my first years in this country. Their wives' cooking brings me back to the warm feeling of having a home in America during my first few years in the country. Being 8,000 miles from home could have been a very lonely, scary experience if not for guys like Coach Milhon, who's now in his 80s, and Coach Franson, who's in his late 70s. When I came to this country, I'd recently lost my mom, and it was scary for me to be leaving my dad. Those guys filled the role of father figures for me, and now that my dad has been gone for more than 30 years, they still fill that role for me. I love them dearly.

Another person I'm still close with? Patrick Anukwa, the track coach for the Enugu state team who told me that discus would be my best sport and started me down the path of being a world class discus and hammer thrower. Without Anukwa I wouldn't have even thought of leveraging my athletic talent to broaden my horizons. I'd stayed in touch with him. He's another guy who reminds me of my dad but in a more literal way: the way he talks, the pitch of his voice, the speed of his speech. Hearing him talk is comforting to me. In 2009 he moved to America, initially to Chicago, where his daughter was, to work as a security guard. We talked on the phone a bunch, and one day he told me, "Chris [he always used to call me 'Chris'] it's too cold here. We're from Nigeria. We're not built for this!"

After that I offered to bring him out to California and have him stay at my place to see how he liked the Golden State. I told him I knew a lot of people who owned companies and I could set him up with a job. He came out and he loved it. He moved out here permanently in 2017 and works for a friend of mine as a security guard, a job he loves because he gets to talk to people all the time. I talk to him every week. It makes me feel good that I was able to help a guy who helped me so much.

I'm blessed to have such wonderful friends. I'm surrounded by good people who support me and have similar values to me, and many of them are huge supporters of my foundation. I've gotten to know so many good, interesting people through my charity work like Stan Ross and my friend Shane Cordes in Kansas City and tribal chairman Darrell Mike of the Twenty-Nine Palms Band of Mission Indians in California. Two Native American

casinos—the Morongo and the Yaamava' Resort and Casino at San Manuel—
are great supporters of my foundation.

When you have success in sports—or in any field that has glamour and
fame—you notice that many people want to be your friend, and it becomes
hard to know their intentions. Do they actually value you as a person or
do they just want to be close to your fame? It can feel very isolating, and
through the years, many people have disappointed me, which is crushing.
When you're in my position, you learn a lot about how to read people. You
learn to spot the signs of someone who's selfish or inauthentic. Decades later,
I know who my true friends are and I'm grateful for them.

My friends are an extremely diverse group, which makes sense considering where I come from and where life took me. What I've learned is that
from Africa to Kansas City and everywhere in between, most people are
good. Most people want the same things. They want to take care of their
loved ones, help others, earn a decent living, laugh, treat people kindly, and
enjoy this big, beautiful world.

My life has been quite a journey. From the time I was six years old,
walking along a dirt road in Nigeria for an entire day to escape the war
front, I never quite knew where I'd wind up. But at every turn, wherever
I wound up was always interesting. I developed the ability to adapt, to go
with the flow, to stay positive, and, most importantly, to see the best in
people. Is it a life that most readers of this book can relate to? In some
ways no, but in the most important ways, yes, I believe. We all face difficult circumstances. We all face unexpected challenges. And we all, if we
pay close enough attention, get unexpected opportunities. I'm proud to say
I made the most of mine.

20

THE ATWATER HIT

My good friend Eric Dickerson always used to tell me, "If you play long enough in the NFL, someone's gonna get you." He was right. On a *Monday Night Football* game on September 17, 1990, Denver Broncos safety Steve Atwater got me. He was a great safety who knew how to channel every ounce of his strength into delivering a blow. On that play, which was a run right up the middle, I remember being tired from running the ball a bunch and I wasn't quite bringing it through the hole like I normally did. I picked the wrong play to do that.

Really, it's just timing. Sometimes one guy catches another guy off guard. If the timing is just right—if a guy's center of gravity is high at that exact moment—you can make him look really bad. That's what Atwater did to me.

But while it looked like a devastating hit and the collision was loud on TV, it wasn't especially painful. I popped right up and felt perfectly fine. I had no idea at the time it would become such a thing and that it would be so overblown. Now people talk about it like it was some defining moment, saying I was never the same after that hit. That's just not true. There were too many plays to count that actually did cut into my effectiveness, but that play wasn't one of them. It just got blown up because it took place on *Monday Night Football*, the camera angle was just right to show me going backward, and the Kansas City Chiefs–Broncos rivalry was so intense. Now it's all over YouTube.

I've never talked to Atwater about it, but I heard an interview he gave not long ago when someone asked him about it. The interviewer was teeing Atwater up to gloat about it, but he didn't take the bait. He downplayed the hit and he noted that at the time I was going through a lot of things personally, referring to the death of my newborn son Michael in July of that year. I've always appreciated that he was so gracious. I hadn't been aware that so many people knew about my son and I'm grateful for Atwater's decency. It shows that despite the violence of football most of the guys out there are good people, including Atwater, one of the most ferocious tacklers of all time.

By the way, Atwater's in the Hall of Fame. He's one of the best safeties of all time. There's a lot more to his career than that one play, but when people talk about Atwater, the conversation always comes back to that one play—just like it does with me. So that's that, and I don't think about that moment too much, but it's still something people talk about all the time. It's a little annoying, I guess, but I don't really mind.

Just recently, I was about to board an airplane, and one of the baggage guys came up to me on the gangway right before I was about to board the plane. He had come up from the runway because he'd seen my bag. "I wanted to come over and ask you about what happened with that Atwater hit," he said.

I chuckled to myself. Football fans are crazy. "Okay, what do you wanna know about it?" I said.

He said, "What happened?"

I said, "Football happened!"

The hardest hit I ever took wasn't from Atwater. It was from Richard Dent. It was in 1990, and we were in Chicago playing the Bears and that fearsome defense. Dent and I collided head to head with all our force going in opposite directions. I got knocked silly. For years I had assumed I got the worst of the blow until I found out years later that we *both* suffered the consequences from it. After we had both retired, Dent and I were at an event in Las Vegas, and someone asked Dent what the worst concussion he ever got was. He told the story of that play. It turns out that after the play, Dent had followed my teammates into the Chiefs huddle until one of our offensive linemen said, "Richard, your huddle's over there."

Dent said that when he lined up on the next play he was praying we wouldn't run the ball in his direction. Meanwhile, I couldn't see out of my right eye, and my head was ringing for a few minutes. Steve DeBerg called a running play to me on the very next play, but I said, "Steve, I can't do it. Call something else."

Did Dent or I take ourselves out of the game? Did the trainers look at us? Of course not. That's just how it was in those days and frankly still is. Thinking about your own safety is seen as a sign of weakness. There's always the guy on the bench ready to take your spot. There are many things the NFL has done to improve player safety. But nothing can change the fundamental brutality of the game.

The most disturbing thing I've ever seen on a football field occurred during the last year of my career in 1992. We visited the New York Jets in New Jersey for a late-season game. On a play in the third quarter, Dave Krieg stepped up to avoid a sack, and two of their defensive linemen collided. One of them, Dennis Byrd, fractured a vertebra. He was down on the field for what seemed like hours. He was paralyzed from the waist down. Paralysis—every football player thinks about it, and if they tell you they don't, they're lying. We're human, too.

But after Byrd's injury, we kept playing. We'd just witnessed a human tragedy, the nightmare we all have, but as football players, we're so programmed that we went back out there and played. The mentality of the game doesn't allow for fear when you're out on the field. If you have fear in your head and your focus is compromised, that's when you're going to get hurt. When I heard about Buffalo Bills safety Damar Hamlin collapsing on the field in Cincinnati and I saw that horrifying video, my mind immediately flashed back to that terrible day in New Jersey.

*   *   *

The game is brutal but it's also beautiful. Athletes have a different perspective. We're in the battle. We're not thinking about admiring the talent of the other players. But sometimes we can't help it. Derrick Thomas and Neil Smith come to mind. I just loved watching those guys. I saw them prepare all week. It was a friendly competition between them, like iron sharpening iron. And come Sunday, it was showtime. I was playing in the game, but I still enjoyed the show.

I didn't see Lawrence Taylor that often, but the few times I did, he made quite an impression. His ferociousness and the reckless abandon he played with were like nothing the NFL had seen before or has seen since. Nobody who was as big as him was nearly as quick as him; nobody who was as quick as him was nearly as big as him. And nobody in the history of the sport played with the kind of energy he did, flying around the field like he'd been set on fire. He was unique. The guy could completely destruct an offense singlehandedly from the outside linebacker position.

Another guy I didn't see often but loved watching when I did: Barry Sanders. He was like Houdini. No matter how many tacklers surrounded him, he somehow found a way to escape. How could you not enjoy watching a guy like that?

My friend Eric Dickerson didn't run; he glided. It seemed like he wasn't trying at all, and when you've played in the NFL, you realize how impressive that is. Dickerson made it look easy, and for that reason, I don't think people appreciate just how great he was.

I also loved watching Bo Jackson. The Raiders were our hated rival—Marty Schottenheimer in particular hated the Raiders with a passion—but how can you not enjoy watching Jackson run? He was a complete freak with speed and explosiveness unlike anybody else. If you gave him a small crease, he'd be gone for a touchdown. He was that much of a threat. I loved watching him play baseball when he was a Kansas City Royals outfielder, playing across the parking lot. And even when he was playing for the enemy Raiders, I loved watching him play football.

Jackson's home football stadium—the Los Angeles Memorial Coliseum—was my favorite playing field in the league. It hosted the 1984 Summer Games, and part of me thinks I was destined to enjoy playing there after missing the 1984 Olympics. (The Raiders' soft run defense helped, too.) At the Coliseum the weather was nice, and the grass was well-maintained. It was dry, so it didn't get muddy and slippery.

San Diego would have been in the running for one of my favorite stadiums, but when we played the Chargers at the beginning of the year, Jack Murphy Stadium would still have the dirt infield for baseball. It's insane that professional football players had to deal with that. The dirt was rock hard, and when you'd get tackled, the sand would come right into your eyes and mouth. I felt I needed to wash my face every time I got tackled there.

But those fields were still better than the AstroTurf ones. The worst three stadiums were Seattle's Kingdome, Houston's Astrodome, and Philadelphia's Veterans Stadium. I separated my shoulder in Seattle in 1989 when I tripped on a fold in the turf. The turf at those places was old and worn down; whatever cushion you'd get at a place like Arrowhead Stadium, which wasn't much, didn't exist there.

Nowadays, the artificial turf is much better than the rug on concrete we used to play on, but artificial surfaces are still worse than playing on grass, and the National Football League Players Association is campaigning to make all fields grass. I support them 100 percent. It's inexcusable that NFL players play on sub-optimal surfaces. The sport is dangerous enough already. You'd think NFL owners wouldn't want to subject their multimillion-dollar assets to such risk, but that's the mentality of NFL owners. They don't give a shit about the players. I guess they figure that the players are easier to replace than the field.

21

Back at Arrowhead
and the Super Bowl

On January 1, 2023, I went to see the Kansas City Chiefs host the Denver Broncos. We needed a win to keep alive our chances of getting the No. 1 seed and a first-round bye. The Broncos were having an off year, and we were as good as ever, but in an AFC West rivalry game, anything can happen.

I have season tickets to the Chiefs and come to Kansas City to see them play once a month at least. I stay at the Westin at Crown Center, which is downtown and across the street from beautiful Union Station. That grand old train station is lit up in red after a Chiefs victory and it's also where Kansas City hosted the 2023 NFL Draft. I left my room for the January game at about 9:30 AM, and the lobby was packed with people in Chiefs gear. They had come to Kansas City from all over the Midwest, all over the country really, and they're eating their breakfast or hitting the hotel bar despite the early hour. The jerseys were out in full force: Patrick Mahomes, Travis Kelce, Chris Jones, Derrick Thomas. No Christian Okoye jerseys that day, but I've seen plenty of those in this lobby before.

My friend Meredith Little drove me to the game, and we pulled into the Harry S. Truman Sports Complex off I-70, right next to Kauffman Stadium, where my teammates and I used to go after practice to watch Bo

Jackson play baseball. The Kansas City Royals organization is trying to build a new stadium downtown, but I hope they stay here because this area is a magical place rich with history and memories. This sports complex connects generations; it's sacred ground to Kansas City sports fans.

On this day it happened to be unseasonably warm in Kansas City—temperatures in the mid-50s—and the tailgate scene was rocking when I got there about 90 minutes before the game. The smell of meat and fire filled the air. It's the smell of good barbecue by people who know their barbecue. It's the smell of families and people coming together. It's the smell of anticipation and the belief that this Sunday—like so many Sundays since Andy Reid became the Chiefs' head coach—was going be a good day. It's the smell of people excited that they get to watch the great Patrick Mahomes.

People looked at me when they passed me. They followed me with their eyes, trying to place me, though most don't. But they knew I was an athlete even at age 62, even though my posture is stiff because of my spine problems, and my steps are ginger when I walk. Not many people in that parking lot were my size, and not many were Black. They saw me and thought, *He must be someone—but who?* But by that point, I had left. A guy sitting at a small tailgate drinking a beer eyed me for a moment, then yelled out with excitement, "Christian Okoye!" and pointed at me in a salute.

I waved and said, "What's up, man?"

And then I kept moving along. It's all a little weird, sure, but I'm honored and grateful to mean something to these people.

I was headed to a tailgate in Lot J. The organizers hit me up on Facebook in 2021, and I finally got around to going in 2022, and they're great people as I suspected. Someone at the tailgate made chili with brisket as opposed to ground beef, and it's delicious. They ladled it to me and my two friends

I took to the game and offered us a full bar of drink options, though I declined the alcohol because it's early and I'm not a big drinker. I enjoy having a couple of beverages, but the culture of getting drunk recreationally—of trying to get drunk—doesn't exist in Nigeria and will always be foreign to me.

At the tailgate the photo requests started coming. They're always a little sheepish. *Can…can I take a picture with you?* (I never say no, but once you take that first photo, the ice is broken, and a pack forms, and you're never quite sure when you'll be able to leave.) People saw me posing and came over. They knew I was a former player, but they didn't know who. I heard whispers of people telling their friends: "Christian Okoye…" The pack surrounding me got bigger.

Then we entered the stadium. I usually don't sit in the seats I've purchased; rather, I spend most of my time in a suite owned by my friend Stan Ross. On my walk to the suite, I saw all the stadium employees whom I've been seeing for years, many of whom are now elderly. These are my people, and I make sure to greet them and chat with them. Again, what I love about football isn't the game itself; it's the relationships and, even now as a fan and a Chiefs alumnus, it's the relationships that keep me coming back to Arrowhead year after year. These people are a part of my life in football.

After getting to the suite, I see Ross. He's a smalltown boy from Southern Kansas who made it big as an entrepreneur, owning a company that makes body cameras for police officers. He's very personable, the type of guy who shows that being successful in business is often about treating people the right way. He is down to earth, funny, comfortable in his skin, and is genuinely curious about people, addressing everyone in his suite like they're the most important person in the room. His downfall is that despite going to nearly every Chiefs game he's a huge Raiders fan, going back to the time his father took him to a Chiefs–Raiders game in the 1970s, and the Raiders won. Those were the Raiders of John Madden, Ken Stabler, Ted Hendricks, and all those other crazy guys, and Ross is nothing if not loyal. To this day, every Sunday at Arrowhead, he wears a Raiders T-shirt under his Chiefs gear. The next week I traveled with Ross to Las Vegas to watch the Chiefs play the Raiders.

Such a compassionate guy, Ross is a big supporter of many charities, including mine. He has sponsored multiple charity events for my foundation. I met him at a golf tournament after my career, just like I met my close friend, Bob Clift, who works as a vice president for the STRAT Hotel in Las Vegas. Clift's an extremely warm guy with a great outlook on life; he laughs at everything, and when you're around him, that laugh makes you feel like everything is going to be okay. He's a great supporter of my foundation as well because he cares about people. When I had cancer, Clift was going through some tough times. His wife passed away in 2020, and we've leaned on each other during those tough times, and that made us closer.

There were some other former athletes in the suite. Brian McRae, the former Royals player, is a friend of Ross', and we have mutual friends in common from Kelly's bar, the Kansas City sports bar and institution. McRae is friends with Pat Mahomes, the former Major League Baseball pitcher and father of Patrick Mahomes. Pat Mahomes stopped by our suite with Scott Erickson, the former MLB pitcher who was teammates with Pat when they played for the Minnesota Twins. That's the best part about sports: as the years go by, the wins and losses become less and less important. What lasts are the relationships.

* * *

Arrowhead Stadium is the best stadium in the league. I have no idea how it gets so loud. Is it the acoustics or the fact that Kansas City Chiefs fans care more than any other fanbase? Every Sunday is a party, a chance for an entire region to come together and feel good about itself. The noise comes from the heart. When the Chiefs ran onto the field against the Denver Broncos, the place went berserk. It's a beautiful day, the Chiefs were 12–3, the Broncos were struggling—what's not to like?

Patrick Mahomes led the Chiefs to a touchdown on the first drive of the game. There's nobody like Mahomes. He's beautiful to watch, an athlete who's an artist at heart, who brings creativity to the game. When I was playing, John Elway was the closest thing to what Mahomes is now. Elway scrambled and made throws nobody else would even *think* to attempt, and Mahomes is the same way with the arm angles he throws from, the touch he puts on the ball—like a point guard in basketball—the scrambling in unexpected directions to keep plays alive. He's the type of athlete you'll tell your grandkids you once saw play, and on this day, Mahomes surpassed 5,000 yards passing on the season for the second time in his career, becoming the third quarterback to do so after Tom Brady and Drew Brees.

His top target, of course, is Travis Kelce, who caught seven passes on the day. Kelce is a freak. You just don't see guys his size move with that kind of agility, and defenders can't keep up with how much ground he covers with his long strides and how quickly he changes directions. Whenever the Chiefs need a big first down, everyone knows the ball is going to Kelce, but there's nothing they can do about it. It reminds me of what Marty Schottenheimer would say about our running game back in the day: "The defense knows it's coming, even the fans know it's coming, but still nobody can stop us."

I enjoyed the game from the suite. It's a social scene, and these days everyone's in a good mood because the Chiefs are winning, and each game is a chance for Kansas Citians to feel civic pride. A couple of rows in front of us, a man wore an Okoye jersey; he had no idea I was 10 feet away. I chatted with some friends, was introduced to more people than I can count, and posed for a bunch of pictures.

The Chiefs cheerleaders came out, and someone asked me with a mischievous look in his eye: "Did you ever?"

"Just one time," I said. "I was a good boy." Everybody laughed.

I wore my Chiefs Super Bowl ring. The team gave it to me after the 2019 championship season because I'm one of the Chiefs Ambassadors, the charitable group, and it means a ton to me because it shows that the organization values us. It's a tremendous gesture of respect, typically gracious from the Hunt family. Everyone in the suite was interested in it. They wanted to try it on, to see how big it was on them. They studied it, looking at the diamonds, which are used to make the Chiefs' arrowhead logo and two Vince Lombardi Trophies for the two Super Bowls the Chiefs have won. (The Chiefs, of course, now have a third trophy.)

A lot of people told me how good I looked appearance-wise, considering how long ago I played, and in some ways, that's true. I eat well and take care of myself. My skin is youthful, my teeth are good, and I don't have a pot belly like most guys my age. But beneath the surface, my body is more ravaged than most people can imagine. These comments are well-intended, but they show how people can't truly wrap their heads around what football players go through. "You look great!" they say, and it makes them feel better that after all the bruising hits Christian Okoye looks better than most guys his age. If only they knew. If only they wanted to know.

Still, I enjoyed the social contact, and I enjoyed watching the Chiefs. The offense has been incredible for years, and it's hard to argue with anything Andy Reid (and former offensive coordinator Eric Bieniemy) did, but my one complaint was that they should run the ball just a *little* more. Let those offensive linemen play downhill, give the defense something else to think about, and take a little pressure off Mahomes. What can I say? I learned NFL football at the foot of Marty Schottenheimer.

In this game the Broncos put up a good fight, and the game unexpectedly turned into a struggle for the Chiefs, who fell behind 17–13 in the third quarter. It also turned into a struggle for Mahomes himself, who threw an uncharacteristic interception in the end zone. After the game he told the media that he didn't have his "best stuff." But we scored two touchdowns in the fourth quarter to turn the deficit into a 27–17 lead and held on to win 27–24.

It's another good day for the Chiefs.

*   *   *

My hotel was steps away from Jack Stack, the renowned barbecue place located in the Freight House, the historic railroad building. People often ask me what the best barbecue is in Kansas City, and I often disappoint them because the fact is I like them all. Jack Stack, Q39, Gates, Joe's, Arthur Bryant's—they're all incredible, at least to the palate of this Nigerian. But these days the Jack Stack Freight House location is my spot, and the staff there treats me very well. And while I'm 62 years old and try to eat healthy, you can't beat those burnt ends.

I ate a delicious meal, and as I left the restaurant, a young employee smoking a cigarette outside yelled out, "Christian Okoye!" and waved. The guy couldn't have been older than 25, which means I retired several years before he was born. But that's Kansas City for you: they know and respect their Chiefs history.

After dinner I headed back to the hotel. I planned to meet Britaney Wehrmeister, a friend who does public relations for my charity events. I sat down in the lobby to wait for her, but there's a woman across from me in one of those big, comfortable seats who's wearing a Kansas City Chiefs shirt and had a towel on her hand streaked with blood. She's in her 50s or 60s and was obviously very drunk. I asked her what's going on, and while I didn't quite understand the details, the upshot was that after a long day of drinking, which was centered on the Chiefs game, she had just broken a glass and cut her wrist. She briefly removed the towel and I saw a deep, wide gash, and dark blood was coming out. It's a serious wound, and I worried she didn't understand just how serious it was. She's mostly upset the bartender made her put down her drink and seek help, which she had done by calling her daughter. The plan was that her daughter would take her to the hospital.

So I was waiting for Wehrmeister, and this woman was waiting for her daughter, and we're seated across from each other. She had no idea who I was and asked me if I live in Kansas City. I told her I don't but that I come here all the time. At a certain point, we parted ways; I was under the impression her daughter would pick her up, and she'd get the treatment she needed. This American culture of getting as drunk as possible to best enjoy something is something I'll never understand.

I met my friend Wehrmeister. It turned out her mother's boyfriend is a huge Chiefs fan and a season-ticket holder for years. He really wanted to meet me but didn't want to bother me. I said I was, of course, happy to talk to the man, and he's a very nice guy who's appreciative and respectful.

Sports brings out such a huge range of behavior in fans. Sometimes fans can be cruel and dehumanizing, booing struggling players and making them feel worse than they already do during low moments. But you also see the best of people as well, and as a popular ex-athlete who has forged a connection with Kansas City, I see this side of people a lot.

It's interesting the way people look at me when they meet me for the first time. For years they have looked at me like a god, someone who represents their hopes. Then, all of a sudden, there I am in the flesh, and for a moment, it's like they're living among the gods. I know that I'm very human; the aches all over my body—not to mention the issues I'm having with my brain—tell me so. But if I can make fans feel special, put them in touch with the best aspects of themselves, and give them a feeling of connection with something larger than themselves, I'm happy to play along.

A bit later at the Westin, I was having a drink in the hotel bar when a man came up to me with two kids. They're cousins; one is from Iowa and one is from Montana, and the whole family—all of whom were wearing Chiefs jerseys—were in town for the game. The kids, who were both younger than 10, have never heard of me, but their parents were giddy and were excited to take a picture with me. Then we met the grandmother and grandfather of the family, who were in their 70s or 80s. They drove to

Kansas City from Iowa and were both emotional about meeting me. The grandmother took my hand in hers in a grandmotherly way and said she and her husband have been Chiefs season-ticket holders for 50 years—even before Arrowhead Stadium existed. In all that time, she said the team from the Marty Schottenheimer era is her favorite because the team stayed together for longer and she felt more connection to the players.

She also loved watching our running game at work. When Arrowhead opened and she and her husband were choosing where to sit, someone had told them to sit behind the end zone because you could see the plays develop and the holes form in a way that you can't from the angles they show on TV. She loved watching our offensive line operate and she loved watching me run through the holes.

When he met me, the grandfather had to hold back tears. His lip was quivering when he talked to me. His family told me that I was his favorite player of all time. To see an elderly man with such a beautiful family become so overjoyed is very moving. For all its flaws, this sport has so much meaning for people. We chit chatted for a bit, and he's a very nice man. Then he pulled me in close because there's something he needed to tell me. "To watch you take the ball and burst through that line," he said, as his voice shook while struggling to get the words out, "it was a thing of beauty."

*   *   *

I went to Super Bowl LVII in Arizona. I wouldn't have missed it for the world. I flew to Arizona a few days before the game and did a bunch of interviews, saying I was confident the Kansas City Chiefs would win. People smiled and nodded, and I could tell they were humoring me. I was either delusional or I was just running my mouth for its own sake, the look on people's faces seemed to say. Everyone thought they knew who the better team was.

But I was pretty sure we would win. We had been through so much and had come out the other side. In the last quarter against the Cincinnati Bengals, when Patrick Mahomes was playing on one leg and we had no receivers, we'd somehow found a way to win. Our team had the confidence of knowing we could handle whatever was thrown at us.

Then Super Bowl LVII started, and the Philadelphia Eagles really out-played us during the first half. Making things worse was that Mahomes aggravated his high ankle sprain, and when they showed those clips of Mahomes wincing on the sideline, I'm sure almost everyone thought we had no chance at all. I'm not gonna lie. I also was discouraged about Mahomes and lost some of my confidence. But I happened to be watching the game in a suite with Jim Kelly, the Hall of Famer and former Buffalo Bills quarterback. Kelly knows a few things about playing through pain and about getting up off the mat after everyone has counted out him and his team. "He'll be fine," Kelly told me. "There's no way he's coming out of this game."

Kelly was right. Mahomes was spectacular in the second half. It was amazing to watch.

If Mahomes stays healthy for the rest of his career, he'll be the best ever. He's been a starter for five years and he's taken us to the AFC Championship Game every year. Ever since the guy hit the field, he has played at an MVP level. It's almost as if he's too great to fully appreciate.

As amazing as Mahomes is, you can't overlook that Andy Reid helped him out by staying with the running game in the second half. Our offensive line dominated up front, and Isiah Pacheco ran hard; I like that kid a lot. This Chiefs team the past few years hasn't been known for its rushing attack the way our team was when I played, but the Super Bowl showed that no matter how much the game has changed, its physical aspect will never be completely phased out. To me, our dominance on the ground in the second half felt like a little hat tip to the Martyball era. We're all Chiefs—connected through time.

I was elated when we won. In a way, it felt even better than when we won three years prior because everyone had counted us out. After the game there were all these parties and afterparties in Arizona, but I was exhausted and I moved up my flight to get back to California. Leave the partying for the young people. Leave playing football to the young people.

On my way to the airport, my phone was blowing up with people wanting me to get them into this or that afterparty. I felt all that excitement from afar. I flew home with a huge smile on my face. The guys in the Chiefs locker room deserved this. Chiefs Kingdom deserved this. And I'm forever part of Chiefs Kingdom.

ACKNOWLEDGMENTS

There are so many people who have helped me along the way to thank. Without these people, I wouldn't have lived the life I did. Without these people, this book would not exist. First, my family. My father, Benedict Okoye, whose love and wisdom is with me every day even years after his passing. The same goes for my mother, Cecilia Okoye, who taught me the values of resourcefulness and hard work. My parents somehow put food on the table and clothes on our backs every day and, despite our circumstances, they created a household of happiness.

I could not have asked for a more supportive (and fun) group of siblings: Benedeth, the late Stanislaus, Loretta, Emmanuel, Chikwelu, Obiageli. I love you all.

Patrick Anukwa, the former track coach of the Enugu state track team, was the first coach who saw serious potential in me. He was the first person to tell me there was a future in sports for me.

Innocent Egbunike has been a great friend for decades. Without Egbunike, I wouldn't have come to America. Egbunike was part of a wonderful group of track teammates and lifelong friends I made at Azusa Pacific University, along with Cres Gonzales and the late Blackman Ihem.

I was blessed throughout my sports career to have amazing coaches who were also high-quality people with great values. At Azusa my track coach Terry Franson and my football coach Jim Milhon took me under their wings when I was a kid trying to acclimate to a completely different environment. They became father figures to me.

So did Marty Schottenheimer, who trusted me to become the focal point of the Kansas City Chiefs' offense and taught me what it meant to be a pro. In Kansas City I was lucky to be coached by two running backs coaches who worked constantly with me on the subtleties of the game and became great friends: Bruce Arians and the late Billie Matthews.

Carl Peterson is a terrific general manager who built the Chiefs' playoffs teams in the 1990s. But more importantly he is a good man who always treated me like a human being as opposed to a commodity.

And, of course, there wouldn't be a Nigerian Nightmare without all my football teammates through the years. Starting in college, when I didn't know the rules of this sport, and into the pros, where I knew less about football than anyone else I was playing with, my teammates were always helpful and kind. There are way too many of them to list, but I'm honored to know so many terrific athletes who were even better human beings. My favorite part of football was the friends I made. (A special shoutout here to the offensive linemen I played with.)

A handful of friends from the Chiefs remain some of my best friends: Barry Word, Steve DeBerg, and Jonathan Hayes.

Eric Dickerson has been an extremely loyal friend ever since we met at the 1989 Pro Bowl and he made fun of my Zubaz pants. It was Dickerson who connected me to my cowriter and friend, Greg Hanlon, who worked very hard to understand and convey where I come from and what has shaped me.

Other close friends of mine have supported me in all kinds of ways: Chris Hale, Brad Booth, David "Red" Cross, Bob Clift, Tammy Neros, and Meredith Little.

My charity, the Christian Okoye Foundation, is the most important part of my work life, and Stan Ross, Shane Cordes, and chairman Darrell Mike of the Twenty-Nine Palms Band of Mission Indians have been huge supporters of the foundation as well as friends. Britaney Wehrmeister has helped my charity immensely with events.

Thank you to the late Lamar Hunt, Clark Hunt, and the entire Hunt family. You are the reason the Chiefs do everything with class.

Thank you to Chiefs Kingdom. You gave meaning to everything I did on the field. You are the best fans in the world.

Lastly, but most importantly, my children, who inspire me every day. This book is for them.

Tiana, Kosi, and Laylah: you are my whole world. I love you more than anything.

—Christian Okoye

Thank you to Christian Okoye for trusting me to help tell his incredible life story and for being so honest and insightful. Christian, if your egusi soup is as good as you say it is, I can't wait to try it.

Christian and I wouldn't have met if not for Eric Dickerson, our mutual friend, who's extremely perceptive about people and knew we'd make a good partnership.

Josh Williams, who acquired this book for Triumph Books, believed Christian's story was worth telling. We couldn't have asked for a better editor than Jeff Fedotin, who knows more about the Kansas City Chiefs than anyone on the planet.

Thank you to Dr. Gloria Chuku, chair of Africana studies at the University of Maryland, Baltimore County, for being so generous with her time and educating me about the Igbo people.

Thank you to Corey Langerfeld, sports information director at Azusa Pacific University, who went above and beyond in digging up Christian's records and providing excellent photos.

My colleagues at *People* magazine inspire me every day with their professionalism, work ethic, and dedication to their craft. In particular, the crime team for the year I spent on this book: Alicia Dennis, Patrick Rogers, Corin Cesaric, Steve Helling, Christine Pelisek, Elaine Aradillas, KC Baker, Tristan Balagtas, and Nicole Acosta.

Thank you to my parents—Judy, Wayne, and Marty—who have always understood that being obsessed with sports and being curious about people and the wider world aren't mutually exclusive. This book is proof.

Thank you to my older brothers, Harv and Nick, for showing me how fun and meaningful sports can be.

Thank you to my in-laws, the Kofflers—Eileen, Peter, Jason, Madison, and Jacob—for supporting me and appreciating how much fulfillment I get from my projects.

Thank you to my children, Eli and Maya, who I know will follow their dreams with the earnestness and passion of Christian Okoye.

Thank you to my wife, Lauren, who leaves it all on field to be the best partner and mom we can ask for. My love, my Law. I love you.

—Greg Hanlon